WILHELM DILTHEY'S
PHILOSOPHY OF HISTORY

NUMBER 592
COLUMBIA STUDIES IN THE SOCIAL SCIENCES
EDITED BY
THE FACULTY OF POLITICAL SCIENCE
OF COLUMBIA UNIVERSITY

WILHELM DILTHEY'S
PHILOSOPHY
OF HISTORY

By WILLIAM KLUBACK

COLUMBIA UNIVERSITY PRESS
NEW YORK 1956

The Columbia Studies in the Social Sciences (formerly the
Studies in History, Economics, and Public Law) is a series
edited by the Faculty of Political Science of Columbia
University and published by Columbia University Press for
the purpose of making available scholarly studies produced
within the Faculty.

TO MY PARENTS

PREFACE

Germany at the beginning of the twentieth century was plagued by skepticism and relativism which threatened to undermine the structure of the human sciences. The age of the great systems had passed. Positivism was exerting a powerful influence on German thought. The widespread employment of the methodology of the natural sciences was threatening to destroy the validity of the human sciences.

One of the first historians to recognize the seriousness of the problem was Wilhelm Dilthey. In order to obviate the grave consequence of the collapse of the human sciences, Dilthey set out to give structure to historical thought. He maintained that world-views are the basic structures in which the external world is perceived. Dilthey demanded that the structure of historical thought arise from life and not be imposed upon it. History, he asserted, can accomplish more than description; history can re-experience and intuit all intellectual expressions.

Dilthey represents the efforts made by German historical scholarship to free itself of positivism. He endeavored to furnish a philosophical justification for the work of the German historical school which arose in the eighteenth century in reaction to the abstract ideas of the Enlightenment and of the French Revolution. Dilthey attempted to create a philosophy of philosophies. Believing history to be inseparable from philosophy, he declared that the historian's task was to grasp the totality of thought and to understand its development and expression. Dilthey maintained that to overcome the one-sidedness and relativity of all thought was to know the meaning of historical consciousness. To envision the phenomena of the moral world as products of historical evolution is historical consciousness. This formulation of a definition of historical consciousness was Dilthey's supreme achievement.

Dilthey set himself the task of writing a critique of historical reason. He wished to submit the historian's procedure to an epistemological examination as Kant had previously examined the procedure of the mathematician and natural scientist. Rejecting metaphysics, Dilthey was determined to prove that all knowledge was derived from experience. He maintained that philosophy arose from life. Life escapes all limitations; it can not be fixed. Fragmentary in character, it manifests itself differently in each moment in the course of historical evolution. Viewing the totality of life, which is possible for the historian alone, we transcend the limitation and relativity of each particular life-experience and thus reconcile ourselves to the great historical forces which history has engendered.[1] The historian is the interpreter of all intellectual expressions; he alone grasps the multiplicity of intellectual life.

Unfortunately, Dilthey's profound formulation of the historian's role and of the essential nature of history has been neglected. His paucity of readers and of critical appraisal is undoubtedly due to his unsystematic presentation. It is not unfair to say that one logically expects from a thinker who proposes a new point of view a clearer and more exact exposition than Dilthey's. There is little organization or unity in Dilthey's writings. Even the titles of his works,

[1] Wilhelm Dilthey, "Traum," in *Gesammelte Schriften*, Vol. VIII.

e.g., "Ideas concerning — —" and "Contributions toward
— —," support this impression;[2] in Dilthey's works themselves one often finds that discussions are fragmentary and
incomplete, that ideas are suggested but never fully developed.

In Dilthey's defense it should be noted that his failure to
achieve a systematic presentation of thought accords with
his view of the fragmentary character of life. "Life should
be interpreted from its own self," was Dilthey's fundamental
thesis. He further argued that the proper historical attitude is to be receptive to whatever life may present at any
moment. He believed that life never reveals itself in its
full significance but emerges in consciousness only partially.

The historian should not expect to find in Dilthey's works
a comprehensive narrative of intellectual history. Dilthey
would not deny the usefulness of such a narrative but would
insist that intellectual history concern itself primarily with
an attempt to grasp intuitively the essential and distinguish-
ing character of each decisive period of intellectual creativeness. He thus limits himself to the development of a methodology and an approach to be employed by the historian
of ideas. He exemplifies this methodology through studies
of selected periods of intellectual creativeness. These studies offer the historian the insight into the methodology and
object of intellectual history.

Dilthey's great contribution to the history of thought was
the demonstration that through historical understanding
man becomes conscious of the totality of all human experience. He succeeded in proving that only the historically
conscious mind could comprehend all philosophical systems.

---

[2] See for example, "Beiträge zur Lösung der Frage vom Ursprung
unseres Glaubens an die Realität der Aussenwelt und seinem Recht," in
Gesammelte Schriften, V, 90.

The historian sees the partial truth of all intellectual expressions and achieves an intellectual freedom which is the highest aim of man. Dilthey realized this achievement only after a lifelong and productive intellectual development which I have attempted to survey in this book.

WILLIAM KLUBACK

Hunter College
New York, January, 1956
New York,
January, 1956

ACKNOWLEDGMENTS

It is impossible for me to express my gratitude sufficiently to all those who have been instrumental in the writing of this book. I am indebted to Professor Jacques Barzun for his guidance and understanding. My debt to Professors Dino Bigongiari, Enrico De'Negri, and Horace Friess is great, for they have influenced my thought, in ways that even they can hardly suspect, through numerous discussions which took place over a period of years. I am grateful to Professors Martin Weinbaum and Gunther Keil, who generously and carefully read the manuscript.

W. K.

CONTENTS

WILHELM DILTHEY'S
PHILOSOPHY OF HISTORY

I

THE YOUNG
DILTHEY

Wilhelm Dilthey was born on November 19, 1833 in the village of Biebrich in the Rhineland. Although the Rhineland is usually thought of as being a Catholic region, Nassau had a tradition of Calvinist rulers. Dilthey's family was intimately connected with this tradition. They traced their ancestry back to the inhabitants of Nassau who fought for freedom in England in the "Glorious Revolution" of 1688, which put the House of Orange on the English throne. His family served the dukes of Nassau for generations as chaplains and councilors.[1] Dilthey counted among his ancestors twelve preachers, seven lawyers, eight government officials in Nassau service, and only three businessmen.[2]

Of his grandparents it was his mother's father, John Peter Heuschhel, who influenced Dilthey most. "Papa" Heuschhel devoted his life to music. He was organist and Kapellmeister at the court chapel at Hildburghausen. When his pupil, Princess Luise, became the wife of the Duke of Nassau, he was called to Wiesbaden as court musician. Carl Maria von Weber was his first pupil. An interest in music, started by his mother and fostered by Papa Heuschhel, led Dilthey to look upon life as a "great symphony, composed by God, which the poets harmo-

[1] Wilhelm Dilthey, *Der junge Dilthey: Ein Lebensbild in Briefen und Tagebüchern, 1852-1870*, ed. by Clara Misch (Berlin, 1933), p. 290.
[2] *Ibid.*, pp. 296-97.

nized." Dilthey's intense feeling for music led him to call it the "greatest of all arts." [3] Some of his happiest moments came when he could play four-handed with Papa or his mother. [4]

The Rhineland was almost as important in Dilthey's early development as was his family tradition. Dilthey was greatly impressed with the charm and order of the Rhenish landscape, the closeness between man and nature in the farms and villages, the nearness of God who seemed immanent in nature. Here in the Rhineland were ruins of castles which told of the glories of the past. Here were sung the songs which made the past not history but part of everyday life. From the Rhineland Dilthey felt he had learned to regard the phenomenal world as symbolic of universal truths and to look behind the appearance for the meaning which gave these truths life. [5]

Maximilian Dilthey, Wilhelm's father, was easy-going and tolerant. He spent many long hours discussing different theological issues with his counterpart in the Catholic Church, Father Eberhard, or with the freethinker, Bernhard May. He brought his children up to be good Protestants, although they attended the Catholic school of the predominantly Catholic Rhineland. He taught them that the theological façade only hid the essential unity of spirit in all religions. [6] He did not want Wilhelm to grow up with a narrow, merely theological understanding of God. To Maximilian Dilthey, God was that force which permeated the universe and gave it life. The Deity was present for whoever would seek Him out. He was to be found in the universe in a great life-giving fashion. The path to understanding Him was through nature and, above all, through His highest creation, man.

[3] *Ibid.*, p. 298.   [4] *Ibid.*, p. 320.   [5] *Ibid.*, p. 302.   [6] *Ibid.*, p. 302.

Although Wilhelm Dilthey left his Rhineland home and his religious family background at an early age, he carried with him, throughout a long and fruitful academic life, that basic pantheistic feeling formed on the walks with his father. The concept of pantheism was central to Dilthey's thought. The exact meaning of the term changed for Dilthey through the years, but the common denominator remained a vague feeling of unity with a universal force which was expressed in all phenomena. As Dilthey first used the term in his Rhineland years, pantheism meant the feeling that there was a unifying force behind occurrences. One could make contact with this universal force by the contemplation of the nature in which it was represented. The connection was made through intuition rather than by an empirical investigation. The basic idea of a pantheistic force in the world was a key to Dilthey's thinking. It was apparent in the earliest thoughts of his youth and set the tone of his world-view throughout life.[7]

Dilthey later expanded his early ideas into a philosophic world-view.[8] At the age of thirteen Wilhelm left Biebrich to attend the Wiesbaden gymnasium. Here his quiet curiosity about the world blossomed under the tutelage of Professor Carl Firnhaber. At this time also came an impetus to a specifically philosophical investigation. In the summer of 1850 Dilthey discovered in his father's library the *Logic* of Immanuel Kant. Kant impressed the youth profoundly. After this first awakening, the Enlightenment ideals of Lessing's *Anti-Goeze* broadened his intellectual horizons still more. Then in the historical analogies of the literary historian G. G. Gervinus, Dilthey found a bridge between cultural history and philosophical thinking. From

---

[7] Herman Nohl, "Der Junge Dilthey," *Germanisch-Romanische Monatsschrift,* XXII (1934), 143.
[8] *Ibid.*

Gervinus Dilthey first learned to understand the writings of individuals as a reflection of their times.

Both Dilthey's growing philosophical interest in universal ideas and his religious background led him into the ministry as a career. With an immense drive to make the multiplicity of the world one in his consciousness, Dilthey began his theological studies at Heidelberg in the spring of 1852. One of his philosophy instructors at the university was the young *dozent,* Kuno Fischer. Fischer was of the left wing of the Hegelian school, composed of a group of young radical thinkers who believed that man and the universe were both rational and that the logic of history would lead to the greater use of man's reason. Fischer also shared Dilthey's central pantheistic outlook in religion. He greatly influenced the young Dilthey, whom he turned to the systematic study of the history of philosophy. Dilthey's later studies of philosophers show the influence of Fischer's clear and penetrating essays on the great personalities of the philosophical world.

Fischer took an interest in Dilthey and introduced him to a circle of intellectuals at the university. However, the earnest Wilhelm could not stand the dilettantism of this group, and for inspiration he turned instead to tramping the Rhenish hills with a copy of Friedrich Hölderlin's poems in his pocket.[9] It was still the Rhineland that Dilthey loved. The emphasis on the world of nature he found in the poetry of the romantics. Hölderlin in particular made a tremendous impression on the Heidelberg student. Here was experienced the same world-view expressed systematically in the idealist philosophy of Georg Wilhelm Hegel. It was from the poet rather than from the philosopher that Dilthey drew his idealism. It was with Hölder-

9 *Der junge Dilthey,* ed. by Clara Misch, p. 114.

lin that the young student linked his experience in nature and the pantheistic connection of all occurrences.[10] In later years Dilthey reaffirmed the idea that one can really understand only like mentalities.[11] That Hölderlin was a like mind was testified by the masterly essay on Hölderlin in *Das Erlebnis und die Dichtung*,[12] which assured Dilthey an honored place among literary critics and historians.

In Hölderlin's poetry Dilthey found the ideas and images which gave form to his own vague religious feelings. During his university years Dilthey began to apply the term pantheism to the idea that there was a universal living idea-force behind all historical occurrences. This life force, functioning through history, gave form and meaning to the incidents of history; it was immanent. Dilthey envisioned a great stream of historical being which nourished society and enabled it to grow.

Dilthey decided to continue his studies in Berlin after learning in the summer of 1853 of Fischer's dismissal by the ministry because of the conservative religious opposition to his pantheism. To the young thinker from the peasant village, Berlin had infinite possibilities. In addition to the best resources for theological studies, Berlin offered the world of art, the theater, and the symphony. There Dilthey could come in close contact with German and West European culture. In the fall of 1853 Dilthey went to Berlin and matriculated in the theological faculty in September of that year.[13]

[10] Eduard Spranger, Introduction to Sigrid von der Schulenburg, ed., "Briefe Wilhelm Diltheys an Bernhard und Luise Scholz 1859-1864," in *Sitzungsberichte der Preussischen Akademie der Wissenschaften, Philosophisch-historisch Klasse* (Berlin, 1933), p. 422.

[11] Dilthey, "Beiträge zum Studium der Individualität" (1895), in *Gesammelte Schriften*, V, 278.

[12] Dilthey, *Das Erlebnis und die Dichtung* (Berlin, 1905).

[13] *Der junge Dilthey*, p. 8.

To supplement his formal theological education during his first term in Berlin, Dilthey entered the circle of Schleiermacher enthusiasts. Friedrich Schleiermacher was the greatest German theologian of the nineteenth century. Adolf Sydow, a *Privatdozent* in theology, first introduced Dilthey to the edition of Schleiermacher's literary papers edited by Ludwig Jonas [14] (Schleiermacher's son-in-law and deacon of the Nicolai Church in Berlin). Dilthey's interest in Schleiermacher led him to an intensive study of the philosopher theologian in his second term in Berlin. He was drawn to Schleiermacher by the latter's philosophy of the universal manifested in the particular. This German romantic theologian saw the main problem of his work to be the reconciliation of the eternal truths of God with the multiple truths of the historical world. Here was a man who could offer answers to the problems with which Dilthey was struggling. In contact with Schleiermacher's philosophy, Dilthey's pantheism and his interest in life and history grew further toward a systematic view.

In Berlin's cultured society Dilthey studied each expression of the human spirit in an effort to understand it scientifically. Particularly in the realm of music was this true. Throughout his stay in Berlin Dilthey attended the Berlin *Sinfoniekapelle* led by Karl Liebig. There he enjoyed most the classical German composers, Johann Sebastian Bach, Joseph Haydn, Mozart, and Beethoven. He studied the characteristics of each composer and the ideas behind the creation of the various compositions,[15] analyzing not only the forms of the musical compositions but the ideas and impressions which they aroused. He investigated the various works as expressions of universal ideas. Dilthey found music everywhere in creation. It was for him an "imita-

[14] *Ibid.*, p. 10.   [15] *Ibid.*, pp. 14, 16, 18.

tion" of a universal harmony which God made into the world. Dilthey always saw musical expressions in relation to the entire human world and to the spirit of the times.[16] Whoever reads Dilthey's great studies of music in the eighteenth century will understand the religious impulse behind music as he saw it. Music was always Dilthey's favorite art expression. As painting and sculpture showed the outer world, so music showed the inner world of the feeling of the composed.[17]

The cultural influences of Berlin made their greatest impression upon Dilthey through the medium of circles of students and professors who met to discuss topics of philosophical and scientific interest in the home of the philosopher, Adolf Trendelenburg, and of the literary critic, Moritz Lazarus. By the middle of the first year Dilthey had wandered from the theological faculty and was attending Trendelenburg's lectures on the history of philosophy.[18] In Trendelenburg Dilthey found the epitome of the scholarly life; in the Trendelenburg household, the young theological student felt at home; from his association with the philosopher, Dilthey drew both material and inspiration for his thoughts about human affairs.

Dilthey had also become a welcome guest on Sunday afternoons at the home of Moritz Lazarus, with whom he studied the Old Testament in the Hebrew and gained an introduction to the works of Baruch Spinoza. This cosmopolitan Lazarus, who was the literary editor of Franz Kugler's *Kunstblatt,* was also conversant with all the latest movements in art in Berlin.

In addition to these two circles, Dilthey studied the

---

16 *Ibid.,* pp. 14, 18.
17 Dilthey, *Von deutscher Dichtung und Musik* (Berlin, 1933).
18 *Ibid.,* p. 19.

Greek philosophers with other young philosophy students.[19] Here, as in his study of music, Dilthey sought to understand the man behind the writings and to find in the writings the feeling for life which gave rise to them. Dilthey enjoyed matching his views against those of others interested in the same problems. "Only in such a life are striving, work, and happiness bound up together," he wrote to his brother.[20]

Dilthey's attraction toward philosophical studies weakened his desire to enter the ministry. By the end of three semesters' work he was convinced that he could not possibly enter the ministry in the state of indecision in which he found himself, and he determined to become a university professor in the theological faculty.[21] He did, however, compromise with his father's desires to the extent that he took the state examination both for the ministry and for teaching in secondary school. He won first place in the theological examination and preached his first sermon in the old Mosbach Church in the summer of 1856.[22]

Dilthey started teaching that same summer, first at the Royal French Gymnasium and then at the Joachimsthal Gymnasium, where he taught intermediate Latin, religion, German, Hebrew, and history.[23] Dilthey had many friends at Joachimsthal. All, like Dilthey, were trying to support the body while they cultivated the mind in further study at the university. Dilthey taught for two years because he depended upon the small income. In the summer of 1858 he was forced to give up the position as a result of persistent sickness and overwork.

The following three years were transitional ones in Dilthey's thought. His earlier religious views were progres-

---

[19] *Ibid.,* p. 31.   [20] *Ibid.,* p. 47.   [21] *Ibid.,* p. 26.
[22] *Ibid.,* pp. 281, 303.
[23] *Ibid.,* p. 303. Both high schools were located in Berlin.

sively secularized by his studies and by his contacts with
the intellectual currents of his times into what might be
called a "life philosophy." As interpreted later by him,
this philosophy was built around the proposition that ideas
grow out of life and influence it because they are in a sense
directly immanent in it. Instead of an omnipresent, immanent God, Dilthey was now coming to believe there was
an overall immanent idea. As in German thought generally, so too in Dilthey, theology was transformed into
idealist philosophy.

✗ In this transitional period Dilthey developed two projects
which had grown out of his studies for the ministry.
Firstly, his concern with early Christianity inspired him to
write an intellectual history of the Middle Ages, both for
its own sake and for a clue to the study of the history of
the human spirit. Secondly, he studied the formative period of the historical, idealist, and liberal world-view in
Germany. In the pursuit of these two interests one can see
the outlines of the philological-idealistic method, which investigated expressions of the human mind in order to arrive at the central ideas behind them. It tried to ascertain
the relationship not only of human expression to the idea
but also of the idea to the life of the times. It was during
this period that Dilthey developed his interest in a critique
of historical reason.

His studies of the Middle Ages were a continuation of
investigations of the world of early Christianity as revealed
in the Pauline epistles, a piece of work which he had undertaken as preparation for the ministry. He proceeded
from this to the study of the period of transition from the
classical to the Christian age. Intensified work on the
Neoplatonists and the early Church Fathers had led in
1857 to a venture into print in Johann Jakob Herzog's

Real-Encyclopaedie für protestantische Theologie und Kirche.[24] Dilthey contributed minor articles and a fifteen-page analysis of the Gnostic Marcion and his school.[25] By the summer of 1860 Dilthey had advanced from an investigation of the patristic period to that of the Scholastics.[26] Of particular interest for him was the pantheistic schoolman, Scotus Eriugena.

It was in April, 1859, that Dilthey outlined his project for a "history of the world-view of the Middle Ages." [27] He wanted to trace the Judaic, Greek, and other influences in the various stages of the development of the concept of the *logos* during this period.[28] Another pattern he wished to follow was that of the emanation systems of the ancient Greeks, of the Jewish-Greek philosopher Philo, and of the Neoplatonists.[29] These emanation systems saw the world as a series of emanations from the original godhead. Still later he attempted to follow Christian poetic types in their various phases of development—types such as the wandering Jew, holy types, Satan, etc.[30] The most successful of these attempts at typology resulted in the study of "Satan in der Christlichen Poesie," which Dilthey published under the pseudonym Hoffner in *Westermanns Monatshefte*.[31]

In writing this "history of the world-view of the Middle Ages," Dilthey felt he would be fulfilling a need for the revival of spiritual values in his own age of materialist controversy. In his diary for November 14, 1860, he considered his life work to be "to grasp the essence of religious life in history and to portray it in our age, which is deter-

---

[24] Johann Jakob Herzog, *Real-Encyclopaedie für Protestantische Theologie und Kirche* (20 vols.; Leipzig, 1847-1888).
[25] *Der junge Dilthey*, pp. 281, 316.   [26] *Ibid.*, p. 104.
[27] *Ibid.*, p. 84.   [28] *Ibid.*, p. 86.   [29] *Ibid.*, p. 84.
[30] *Ibid.*, pp. 130-31.
[31] Dilthey, "Satan in der Christlichen Poesie, eine literarische Studie," *Westermanns Monatshefte*, VIII (1860), pp. 321-29, 434-39.

mined exclusively by the state and by natural science." [32]
He hoped to bring about a revival of religiosity such as had
occurred in the period of transition from the classical
world-view to that of the Middle Ages. At this time there
had arisen a world-view "which tried to do the same thing
we are trying to do: to unite the best aspects of the world-
view of both the Graeco-Roman world and the Middle
Ages." [33] It had combined the religious, poetic, and philosophical points of view with the political and scientific
and had thus given full expression to the human spirit.
"My view on the relation of Christianity to philosophy and
art, my whole passionate love of true Christianity would be
in such a program." [34]

In his study of the Middle Ages, Dilthey developed further the philological techniques of document analysis. He
studied the content of each work of art or literature min-
utely. First, he depicted the whole artistic creation, then
the author, and finally, the age. In the fall of 1860 he
wandered through Cologne, achieving an understanding of
the thoughts and feelings of the men of the Middle Ages
from the architecture and sculpture of the city.[35]

The most important aspect of Dilthey's work on the
Middle Ages was that it was the occasion for his earliest
thoughts on a critique of historical reason. This was to
unite the generalizing spirit of philosophy with the individ-
ualizing view of history, for he had found that "every single
historical occurrence leads to general ideas." [36] He was
working at the point where history and philosophy meet,
continually going back and forth between the two, using

[32] *Der junge Dilthey,* pp. 140-41.
[33] *Ibid.,* p. 40.   [34] *Ibid.,* p. 61.
[35] Dilthey to Bernard Scholz, November, 1860, in Schulenburg,
"Briefe Wilhelm Diltheys an Bernhard und Luise Scholz," p. 449.
[36] *Der junge Dilthey,* p. 175.

each to round out and test the other. He became convinced that the ideal course was to follow both methods
simultaneously. "I want to develop the two plans which
are stirring in my mind," he wrote in his diary a year after
starting the world-view studies. One of these would be
"an historical development of the Christian world-view of
the West"; the other, "a critical investigation of the philosophical and religious spirit arising from an historical grasp
of the genesis of systems. . . ." This method "would be a
new critique of pure reason based on our historical-philo-
sophical world-view." [37]

The work on the Middle Ages thus was beginning to
show the interplay of the two fundamental themes of Dilthey's work. These were: (1) a desire to create an ade-
quate critical method for the study of man's ideas; (2) an
attempt to clarify a metaphysical world-view.

During these transitional years in Dilthey's thought, he
had become interested in the world-view which arose in the
latter part of the eighteenth century. This age was permeated by a religious-historical reaction to the Enlightenment. It partook of the classical and Christian outlooks
and recognized as its major problem the reconciliation of
the two traditions. In an attempt to understand the essence
of the religious life of this time, Dilthey was led to a study
of Johann Georg Hamann [38] and once again to Friedrich
Schleiermacher.[39] The results appeared in two articles in
1859 and 1860. There was a consistent development of
thought leading from Hamann to Friedrich Heinrich
Jacobi, who introduced the pantheist Spinoza to Goethe
and to Germany. Goethe's pantheistic ideas in turn were

[37] *Ibid.*, p. 120.
[38] Dilthey, *Gesammelte Schriften,* XI, 1-33.
[39] Dilthey, "Schleiermacher," *Westermanns Monatshefte,* V, (1859),
602-14.

given philosophical form by Schleiermacher. In the writings of Hamann and Schleiermacher, Dilthey found the uniqueness and independence of religious development studied in empirical fashion. Moreover, these writings afforded Dilthey the opportunity to learn the world-view of an age as a whole in a more immediate fashion than he could know the age of the Church Fathers and the Scholastics.

For his study of Hamann, Dilthey read Karl Hermann Gildemeister's *Hamanns Leben und Schriften*,[40] of which three volumes had then appeared. Hamann, in the pietistic tradition, attacked the rationalism of the Enlightenment. He regarded religion as a factual phenomenon, independent of all abstract thought. He struggled with life to find a basic view which would open "a new way to a universal historical understanding of the primordial, first cause." [41] According to Hamann, nature was the word of God, and things were merely the reflection of hidden ideas. "Nature leads me to the Bible, and the Bible leads me to nature," he wrote.[42] "Nor do our thoughts start with one or the other but out of a complex." [43] Everything man sees or hears is the word of God. Here Dilthey felt at home. Here was expressed his own inner conviction of the historical and pantheistic nature of the universe and of man's culture.

At the same time that the article on Hamann appeared, Dilthey published in *Westermanns Monatshefte* an article on Schleiermacher; he used the pseudonym Wilhelm Hoffner. Dilthey found in Schleiermacher the same romantic-historical-spiritual interpretation which he had admired in Hamann, and in addition he found a method.

---

[40] In 6 vols., Gotha, 1857-73.
[41] *Der junge Dilthey*, pp. 281, 316.
[42] Dilthey, *Gesammelte Schriften*, XI, 12.   [43] *Ibid.*, p. 33.

Schleiermacher continued the critical methodology employed in his analysis of Plato in examining the ideas of Christianity through a study of Paul's letters. The technique of interpreting the works of the human mind, the study of hermeneutics, was the greatest contribution of Schleiermacher to Dilthey's thought. His indebtedness was subsequently shown by the fact that he returned to the great teacher in no less than six independent studies at different times in his life.

Dilthey had a chance to make a deeper study of Schleiermacher's methods of interpretation of the ideas of an age when the Schleiermacher Institute offered a prize for an essay entitled "On the Meaning of the Schleiermacher Hermeneutics in Its Relation to Former Attempts." He was overjoyed at the opportunity this presented to investigate Schleiermacher's historical-philological methods and to compare them with those of the German classical philologist, Friedrich August Wolf, and of the romantic philosopher, Friedrich Schlegel. The essay gave Dilthey a chance to test his own methods of dealing with Church documents by understanding more carefully how Schleiermacher had done so. "All questions which have a connection with the methods of historical intuition have for me an immense charm," Dilthey wrote to his brother. "Here they harmonize with my long interest in Schleiermacher." [44] Dilthey set to work in May, 1859, and worked all the rest of the year on the project. He traced the ideas from Schleiermacher back to their foundations in the ancients. The critical method he traced to Plato, the allegorical to Crates of Mallos.[45] His efforts were crowned in February, 1860, by the prize "in recognition of comprehensive study and thorough investigation." [46]

[44] *Der junge Dilthey,* p. 70.   [45] *Ibid.,* p. 77.   [46] *Ibid.,* pp. 102-3.

Dilthey's interest in Schleiermacher had also led him to help Jonas in the editing of Schleiermacher's letters. When Jonas died in the fall of 1859, Dilthey undertook to complete the work. By the autumn of 1860 the editing of the third volume was completed.[47] From these letters Dilthey drew much material for the understanding of an age. In his study of the letters, he followed many ideas to their sources. This directed him to Schleiermacher's other writings and to the contemporary philosophers, Johann Gottlieb Fichte and Friedrich Schlegel.[48] Dilthey hoped to be able to write a short history of the romantic school from a study of the correspondence among its members. The letters furnished an excellent insight into the more intimate intellectual relationships between the Schlegels, the poets Friedrich von Hardenberg (Novalis) and Ludwig Tieck, and Schleiermacher.[49]

At the same time that Dilthey was becoming alienated from formal theological studies and turning toward a more universal philological-idealistic tradition, he was also deciding his future professional career. The end of the years of transition and the beginning of his new philosophical outlook were symbolized by Dilthey's decision in February, 1861, to leave the theological faculty for the philosophical faculty. Dilthey had fallen decisively under the influence of what he was later to call the key trait of the modern world—the secularization of the predominantly religious orientation of the Middle Ages.

There were three main reasons why Dilthey decided to leave the theological faculty. Firstly, he had come to feel that in the theological faculty he would always have to work within a strictly Christian framework and could not

[47] Wilhelm Dilthey, ed., *Aus Schleiermachers Leben in Briefen,* Vol. III (Berlin, 1860).

[48] *Der junge Dilthey,* p. 67.   [49] *Ibid.,* p. 110.

investigate wherever and whatever he pleased. He had already begun to see religious values in a more universal formulation than the Christian one. Secondly, as he worked on a history of the Christian world-view and dogma, he became disgusted with the sectarian squabbles and hairsplitting. "In reality, all the historian of Christianity experiences is the tortures of Tantalus. I fight continually to win my way to the inner life of this unfriendly material." [50] Finally Dilthey was persuaded to redirect his studies by the fact that early in 1861 a student published a treatise on the logic of the Scholastics which covered the same ground as he had intended to cover and thus rendered Dilthey's work superfluous.

Dilthey never abandoned the theological studies begun early in his life. In a broader sense, he carried on his theological work through his study of Schleiermacher, who became a symbol of Dilthey's new orientation. The attempt to trace Christian types in poetry and in art culminated in Dilthey's concept of poetic types. Moreover, the study of the development of the *logos* and of emanation systems taught Dilthey to understand the developmental history of ideas.

Even more important than the specific knowledge and techniques which Dilthey had acquired during his time as a theological student was the broadening of his conception of the pantheistic nature of things from the natural world to the cultural and historical world. From his youth Dilthey had considered poetry, music, and philosophy of equal value as religion. At Berlin the world of culture and history became the focal point of interest. The reality of religion was immanent not only in the natural universe but

[50] Quoted by Georg Misch in his "Einleitung" (Introduction) to Vol. V of Dilthey, *Gesammelte Schriften*, p. xxiii.

also in man's cultural achievements. The spirit of Christianity reposed not alone in the cross, nor in the theological explanation of it, but rather in the entire expression of Western man. Christianity meant for Dilthey the entire world-view of Western man as expressed in his art, thought, and literature as well as in his religion.

After he determined to leave the theological faculty, Dilthey hesitated a long time before choosing which division of the philosophical faculty to attend. The choice lay between history and philosophy. When Dilthey finally chose philosophy as his field, he explained his choice to his father thus: "I am perhaps too abstract, too much of a person drawn to questions of the mind, to stay in history. The intuition of characters and systems, of the continuities and the analogies in history, is much dearer to me." [51] Although the discipline of history thus lost the nominal allegiance of one of its most creative thinkers, Dilthey's dual loyalty was shown by the fact that he always looked at philosophy from an historical point of view and that the central problem of his philosophy was to furnish a critical philosophical foundation for historical investigations.[52]

[51] *Der junge Dilthey,* p. 30.   [52] *Ibid.,* p. 283.

II

HISTORICISM AND

IDEALISM

To understand Dilthey's scholarly concerns during the 1860's, one must understand the meaning of the term historicism as it was used then. It would seem appropriate to begin defining historicism by quoting from Leopold Ranke's *Dialogue on Politics*. Writes Ranke: "There is an element which makes a state not a subdivision of general categories, but a living thing, an individual, a unique self." This "unique self" was identical with the "idea." In the study of the "unique spiritual existence of the individual state, its principle," the historian rose to "a true perception and appreciation of uniqueness and spiritual difference." His highest aim was a "divining perception of the deeply hidden, all-embracing spiritual laws," of the spiritual substances, original creations of the human mind—the thought of God." And his highest satisfaction was the contemplation of "these many separate, earthly-spiritual communities, called forth by genius and moral energy, growing irresistibly, progressing amidst all turmoil of the world toward the ideal, each in its own way." [1]

The dominating assumption of historicism then as now holds that the methods of the sciences of nature did not apply to the study of human society and culture, as a different kind of subject matter necessitated different methods of

[1] Theodore H. Von Laue, *Leopold Ranke: The Formative Years* (Princeton, 1950), pp. 114-15.

understanding.[2] Instead of supporting the typical Enlightenment belief in a natural law of causation which had universal validity and which could be studied empirically, historicism argued that the free will of the individual, the unique national heritage, and the specific historical situation explained human activities.[3]

Dilthey was influenced by the precepts and ideals of the historical school mainly through personal contacts at the University of Berlin. When Dilthey arrived in Berlin a great many of the early generation of the historical school had died. The philologist Friedrich August Wolf, Wilhelm von Humboldt, the jurists Friedrich Karl von Savigny and Karl Friedrich Eichhorn, the historian Barthold Georg Niebuhr, and the philosopher Schleiermacher were no longer lecturing. This historical school was continued in Dilthey's day by the geographer Karl Ritter, the historian Leopold Ranke, and the philologist August Boeckh.

In his first semester at Berlin, Dilthey attended the lectures on Greek antiquities given by Boeckh, the dean of Germany's classical scholars. A year later, in 1855, Dilthey entered Ranke's seminar in medieval history; the following semester he entered the historian's seminar in modern history.[4] "It is worth much to me to learn Ranke's method," Dilthey wrote his father at this time. "He is still the most important historian." [5]

The basic concepts and methods of the historical school are clearly seen in the thought and writings of these two teachers of the young Dilthey. The starting point of this school was the ascertainment of the facts. Ranke regarded an exact investigation of the facts in their historical setting

---

2 Joachim Wach, *Das Verstehen: Grundzüge einer Geschichte der hermeneutischen Theorie im 19 Jahrhundert* (3 vols.; Tübingen, 1926-1933), I, 187.

3 Dilthey, *Gesammelte Schriften*, III, 145.

4 *Der junge Dilthey*, p. 30.   5 *Ibid.*

to be the foundation of all future understanding in history.[6] He considered each expression of life in history as an original creation of the human spirit, without judging it or comparing it with others. His main aim was to understand it from within, through its genesis and growth, through its maturity and interaction with others, through its mutations to its decline, death, and rebirth in another original creation.[7] He studied the evidence of spontaneous growth as a contemporary understands its freedom of choice at any given moment and also as a retrospective historian sees the underlying necessity, the compulsion of the innate life germ.

The ascertainment of facts led directly to the second level of investigation, a study aimed at a reconstruction of individuals and their psychological motivations from the analysis of the documents in a specific historical situation. Two examples of Ranke's art of characterizing personality are: Maximilian I from the *Histories of the Latin and Teuton Nations;* and Pope Pius V, from the first volume of the *History of the Popes.* According to Ranke's general rule of introducing a historical personality only at the moment of his full impact upon history, the characterization of Maximilian appeared only after a preliminary discussion of his plans as he prepared himself for the Diet of Worms in 1495. At that Diet his personal influence would be the determining factor. That then was the proper place for a sketch of his character.

Ranke began with a general remark, commenting upon the great versatility of Maximilian I and showing how most of the emperor's restless energy was spent in securing and enlarging the Hapsburg family domain. He spoke of the emperor's shrewdness and secretiveness in the pursuit of

6 Wach, *Das Verstehen,* III, 113.
7 Von Laue, *Leopold Ranke,* p. 115.

such plans, and of his ire when he believed his schemes had been discovered.[8]

The characterization of Pius V is more detailed, as was natural in a history of the Popes. That figure had captured Ranke's imagination at an early time. In a letter from Berlin (1827), the young historian commented on him in the clearest evaluation of personality he ever wrote: "Such a pious man, naive as a child, and yet the strictest inquisitor and persecutor of the Protestants who, as regards the essence of his convictions, so closely agreed with them. That shows how much man is subject to error, how weak morally, a fool—and in his weakness great, at time noble even when he is most repulsive. But above all it behooves us to be mild and good. Error will always creep in." [9]

The third level of investigation was the understanding of leading ideas by means of an empirical study of their concrete manifestations—whether it be a work of art, a person, a nation, an epoch—and the recognition of these ideas as the formative influence upon the individual studied. According to Ranke's philosophy of history, the subordination of the individual to the general context was indicative of the individual's position in history. Man was free; else, Ranke would not have given so much attention to the character of each of his historical figures. But he was also subject to the great forces of history. At the most, man could give expression to the "idea," even guide it. But he could never have the power to command it. Man was shown his proper place by the superior forces of universal history. As Ranke commented on the end of Pope Paul III, "How impotent, how insignificant does even the most exalted of mortals appear when placed in contrast with the grand and ceaseless course of events.—He departs, but the destinies of

8 *Ibid.*, p. 133.   9 *Ibid.*, p. 134.

humanity make no pause; they move on to their completion."[10] Boeckh also emphasized the idea behind a civilization, which he regarded as an individual as Ranke had so regarded an epoch. The purpose of philological investigation was to understand the leading ideas behind the political, social, artistic, religious, and philosophical life of a given civilization and eventually to arrive at the central idea which characterized that civilization.[11]

The most important application of this third level of investigation was the study of the *Volksgeist,* or idea of the nation, and its organic growth. This doctrine was of particular importance to the members of the historical school. Its best representative was the jurist Savigny. The historical school argued that the intelligible social unit was not a group of people who made a contract but that group which had grown up together historically and which had evolved the same cultural traditions, laws, and ideals. Barthold Niebuhr created a new national history of Rome; Boeckh showed the unity of life of the ancient Greeks; Jacob Grimm pictured the total view of the old German life; and Ranke argued that the spirit of each nation determined the course of the development of the institutions, laws, and ideals of that nation. Every nation, therefore, evolved its own constitutional structure and could not borrow it from another nation.

Complementing the historical school's emphasis upon intuitional understanding was the view of the Heidelberg and Prussian schools that history was the educator of national morale. Although Dilthey learned his methodology from Ranke and Boeckh, Dilthey's views were closer to those of the leaders of the Heidelberg and Prussian schools.

---

[10] *Ibid.,* p. 136.
[11] Conrad Bursian, *Geschichte der classischen Philologie in Deutschland* (2 vols.; Leipzig, 1833), II, 704.

For Dilthey the great educational achievement of German historical science grew out of the spiritual experiences of the German renaissance in general, and out of the Prussian age of reform in the Wars of Liberation in particular —out of "the fight against French hegemony for the freedom of the German political future." [12] It was during the German movement, said Dilthey, that there arose "a succession of precursors who fought for the right to make history a means of national education." [13] From that time until his own, historians employed the double heritage of German idealism and the political power of the Prussian state to emphasize the need for German unity.

Dilthey first started studying the German historians of the above two schools in the spring of 1859. He anticipated writing a series of essays on various historians for Adolf Glaser's *Westermanns Monatshefte*.[14] Two years later the project was still only an idea. He then told Rudolf Haym of it and the latter suggested he write the series for his *Preussische Jahrbücher*. Spurred by Haym's urging and by a desire to interpret Schlosser, Dilthey set down his views on the value of history for the education of Germany and on Schlosser as an historian. Dilthey's subsequent discussions with Haym and the young Prussian national liberal historians, Ludwig Häusser and Heinrich Treitschke, enabled him to clarify many of his ideas.[15] The Schlosser article was the best of the series. Articles on the historians of the Prussian School—Johannes von Müller, Barthold Georg Niebuhr, and Friedrich Christoph Dahlmann—along with a shorter version of the Schlosser appeared over three years later in *Westermanns Monats-*

---

[12] Dilthey, "Johannes von Müller," in *Gesammelte Schriften*, XI, 79.
[13] Dilthey, "Friedrich Christoph Schlosser," in *Gesammelte Schriften*, XI, 164.
[14] *Der junge Dilthey*, p. 64.   [15] *Ibid.*, p. 173.

hefte. It is from these articles that we draw our understanding of Dilthey's approach to historiography.

Dilthey's ideal of the historian became apparent in these essays. Von Müller represented the historian who grasped the essentials of the crisis of his time and who turned then to a study of history, both to draw personal strength therefrom and to set aright the balance of society. He wrote, said Dilthey, that the nation might gain power from this same course.[16] Dahlmann was the historian who made his mark as the educator of youth. Not only did he teach by example through his active political role in the National Assembly at Frankfort in 1848, but he also spent his days thereafter writing historical and political pamphlets inspiring the younger elements of the middle class to unify Germany.[17] With Schlosser, as with Dahlmann, history entered upon the political arena. History was to point the path of moral political action to the nation, indeed to all mankind.[18] Dilthey singled out Niebuhr as the best example of the historian and the patriotic servant of the state. As a director of the Bank of Berlin Niebuhr had raised the money to keep Prussia solvent in 1806. Again, in the Wars of Liberation he had been despatched to Great Britain to obtain a loan. After the Congress of Vienna, he was the first of a series of scholar-ministers in Rome.[19] Dilthey presented his studies of these men as his inspiration to the nation in the years of the new crisis in the middle of the 1860s.

In formulating his own views Dilthey attempted to rec-

[16] Dilthey, "Johannes von Müller," in *Gesammelte Schriften*, XI, 79-80.

[17] Dilthey, "Friedrich Christoph Dahlmann," in *Gesammelte Schriften*, XI, 179, 185.

[18] *Ibid.*, p. 151.

[19] Dilthey, "Barthold Georg Niebuhr," in *Gesammelte Schriften*, XI, 95-99.

oncile the traditional view of the historical school with the reconstructive aims of the Prussian historians. The true historical view, he said, saw history at one and the the same time as a scientific basis for the human sciences and as a means of national moral education.[20] Dilthey found in Wilhelm von Humboldt an ideal representative of such a view.[21] With him Dilthey felt more at home than with most thinkers of his age.

True knowledge of history, said Humboldt, was possible only by understanding the manner in which the great ideas of history objectified themselves through human actions and thus brought about the realization of man's potentialities in history.[22] Thus, the task of the historian was not to be mastered by intellect alone; it required, rather, the constant cooperation of the creative imagination, which alone was able to tie together into a genuine unity the isolated and widely dispersed facts. But the historian's imagination does not attempt to go beyond the actual events; it subordinates itself to experience and to the investigation of what is real.[23] "All historical understanding depends upon the assimilation of the inquirer with the object of inquiry," said Humboldt.[24] But in order to understand, one must have had an experience which enables us to come to the object with a congenial background. His phrase, "in order to understand, one must have already understood"[25] became the foundation of Dilthey's historical interpretation.

Humboldt also held the general educative view of his-

---

[20] *Der junge Dilthey*, p. 189.   [21] *Ibid.*, p. 76.

[22] Wilhelm von Humboldt, "Über die Aufgabe des Geschichtsschreibers" *Abhandlungen der Könglichen Akademie der Wissenschaft zu Berlin, Historisch-Philologische Klasse, 1820-1821* (Berlin, 1822), p. 321.

[23] Ernst Cassirer, *The Problem of Knowledge* (New Haven, 1950), p. 239.

[24] Humboldt, "Über die Aufgabe des Geschichtsschreibers," p. 314.

[25] *Ibid.*, p. 315.

tory. At the age of thirty-five, after serving as Prussian
minister-plenipotentiary in Rome, he was recalled to Berlin
to become Minister of Public Instruction in 1808. At Berlin he had helped to found the University of Berlin, which
was to become the gathering place of those interested in
creating a practical human science. Two years later Humboldt became minister plenipotentiary at Vienna and proceeded to fulfill similar posts for Prussia for another six
years.

During the late 1850s and the 1860s, historicism, as
represented by the historical school and by the reformative
schools, suffered a sharp challenge to its ideals and to its
claims that it presented a true explanation of historical activity. The challenge came from the positivistic philosophy
as advocated in France by the philosopher Auguste Comte
and in England by the philosopher John Stuart Mill [26] and
the historian Henry Thomas Buckle.

As formulated into a doctrine by Comte, positivism was
founded upon the assumptions of mathematics and the bio-
logical sciences. In opposition to the critical idealism of
Kant and his followers, Comte limited knowledge and science to that which can be perceived through the senses.
The ideas which the historicists saw behind occurrences
were flatly denied. "We cannot go behind occurrences,"
he said. "Any existence behind there we cannot know or
must deny." [27] The less philosophy lost itself in the world
beyond, the "transcendent," the more perfect it would become. Philosophy can only reach for and teach a "human
truth," and it attains its goal the more surely when it re-

[26] The presentation of Mill's ideas shows the inadequate and limited
treatment of these ideas in Germany at the time. Mill's emphasis, in
the later phases of his thought, on history and other social factors was
neglected by his German interpreters.

[27] Auguste Comte, *Cours de philosophie positive,* 5th ed. (6 vols.;
Paris, 1893-1894), I, 9.

stricts itself to the world of mankind.[28] Scientific methodology should be limited to the methods of the natural sciences, to concepts of succession, co-existence, and material
cause and effect. The goal of knowledge was not the mere
accumulation of isolated facts but rather the discernment
of general laws of evolution, climatic influence, and social
organization.[29] Finally, history was looked upon as a result of the working of these natural laws through society as
a whole rather than through specific individuals.[30] Out of
positivism there thus grew a mechanistic and collectivistic
concept of man, society, and history which was in direct
opposition to the voluntaristic and individualistic view of
historicism.

Comtean positivism was reinforced by the logic of Mill,
especially by his theory of the human sciences. Mill agreed
with Comte that the human sciences had to be based on
studies of large bodies of individuals whose actions could
be reduced by statistical analysis to natural laws and that
only empirically ascertained activity could furnish data for
scientific knowledge.[31] The backward state of the human
sciences, said Mill, could only be improved by applying to
them the methods of the physical sciences duly extended
and generalized.[32] The starting point of such a scientific
view was an exact psychology, deduced from the physio-
logical functions of the human mind, which set forth the
laws by which successive states of consciousness followed
one another by the law of association.[33]

The most direct challenge to historicism came not from
the philosophers but from the historian Buckle, who at-

---

[28] Cassirer, *The Problem of Knowledge*, p. 244.
[29] Comte, *Cours de philosophie positive*, IV, 17, 145, 287.
[30] *Ibid.*, I, 16, and V, 14.
[31] John Stuart Mill, *A System of Logic, Ratiocinative and Inductive* (New York, 1873), p. 529.
[32] *Ibid.*, p. 521.   [33] *Ibid.*, p. 532.

tempted to set forth in his *History of Civilization in England* a "true inductive science of history by applying to the history of man those methods of investigation which have been found successful in other branches of knowledge." [34] Buckle opposed the belief that chance operated in the world of man; he did not believe that anything was exempt from the natural order and its rigid determinism. He derived his evidence for this uniformity and necessity in human affairs not so much from history as from statistics, which showed that the alleged freedom of the human will is a delusion. Moreover, said Buckle, if one knows precisely the antecedents of a given situation one can predict precisely the outcome.[35] Individual actions of great men were only ripples upon the stream of history as it moved according to its natural laws and were hardly worth studying.

The penetration of these positivistic ideas into Germany was rapid. Their way was prepared by the anthropological point of view of the philosopher Ludwig Feuerbach's *The Essence of Christianity* in 1841, which argued that the limits of human thought were definitely set by experience and that divinity was hence identical with the human conception of it.[36] Mill's philosophy was introduced in the course of the 1840s by the chemist Justus Liebig, and in 1849 Johann Schiel translated Mill's *System of Logic*.[37]

The most important attempt to combat the threat of positivism by reconstructing historicism was that made by Johann Gustav Droysen, professor of history at the University of Berlin. Coming, as did Dilthey, from a religious background, Droysen felt very strongly the crisis in his

---

[34] Henry Thomas Buckle, *History of Civilization in England* (New York, 1934), p. 164.

[35] *Ibid.*, p. 15.

[36] Ludwig Feuerbach, *Das Wesen des Christentums* (Leipzig, 1841).

[37] John Theodore Merz, *A History of European Thought in the Nineteenth Century* (Edinburg and London, 1912), III, 374.

ideals provoked by the inroads of positivism.[38] "Woe to us," he wrote to his fellow liberal Max Duncker, "if the polytechnical misery, which since 1789 had fouled and dried up France, spreads still more the Babylonian mixture of dissoluteness and calculation."[39] Droysen attempted to ward off all attempts to measure history by the standards of science and eventually to reduce it to a science.

In order to destroy the positivist idea that "only microscope and scales are scientific," Droysen in 1852 developed for a lecture course a "methodology and encyclopedia of the historical sciences" which attempted to create a science of history on historical foundations. He continued his attacks on positivism in the second part of his essay published in 1854, "On the Characteristics of the European Crisis" in which he made a sharp distinction between the subject matter and methodology of the natural sciences and the human sciences.[40] The third blow against positivism was directed at Buckle in an article on "The Elevation of History to the Rank of a Science" which appeared in the *Historische Zeitschrift* of 1862. Here Droysen argued that instead of making a science of history Buckle merely used the methods of the natural sciences and entirely missed the consideration of history's own methods of investigation. The particular element which distinguished history from nature, said Droysen, was the fact that history dealt with a moral world, a world of free judgments, which could not possibly be studied through statistics and causal laws as

[38] Hans Rother, *Geschichte und Politik in der Gedankenwelt Johann Gustav Droysen* (Berlin, 1935), pp. 14-16.

[39] Droysen to Max Duncker, July 17, 1852, in Johann Gustav Droysen, *Briefwechsel,* ed. by Rudolf Hübner (2 vols.; Berlin and Leipzig, 1929), II, 120.

[40] Droysen, "Zur Charakteristik der europäischen Krisis" in Johann Droysen, *Politische Schriften,* ed. by Felix Gilbert (Munich and Berlin, 1933), pp. 307-42.

Buckle proposed. Droysen struck out in the direction of
what has been called the "history of ideas" or "intellectual
history." He aimed to equate history with intellectual creation and moral striving.[41]

The aim of the thinkers experiencing the crisis of historicism was not merely to create a picture of the past individual epochs but also to create a synthesis of knowledge
which could offer an effective solution to the social, educational, and intellectual problems of the present. They
studied the past to clarify the present. The men involved
in this crisis were the Halle philosopher Rudolf Haym and
Dilthey himself.

Another characteristic of the crisis was the emphasis that
was placed upon history in its relation to the problem of
the meaning of life. This, again, represented a reaction to
the concrete historical approach, which had separated itself
from life and the creation of any comprehensive or illuminating historical synthesis. While Ranke had concerned
himself with the general problem of meaning and values,
this was certainly not true for most of his successors.[42]
They had very little concept of the role that value judgments had played in the development of European culture.
As a reaction to this lack of appreciation of ideals in history came the view that an age's organic unity could be
understood only in terms of some central fundamental
value characteristic of that age.

The political historians among the national liberals
taught that history must be practical and useful rather than
aesthetic.[43] They emphasized the volitional factors in his-

---

[41] Rudolf Haym's studies of Herder, Humboldt, Hegel, and the romantic school; also Dilthey's study of Schleiermacher.

[42] Ernst Troeltsch, *Der Historismus und seine Probleme, Gesammelte
Schriften* (Tübingen, 1922), III, 4-5.

[43] *Ibid.*, p. 5.

tory rather than the intellectual or contemplative factors and the creative role in writing history rather than the passive reception of an external historical reality. They believed that thought was related to the realm of action in the present.[44]

Dilthey clarified his thoughts about the problems brought forth by the positivist challenge to historicism in two debating circles. Because of the influence of these circles upon Dilthey and because Dilthey's reaction to them furnishes an excellent insight into his own views on the nature of history, they will be discussed below at some length.

The first of the circles was that which met Sunday afternoons at the home of Moritz Lazarus. During the three years, 1857 to 1860, Dilthey was a weekly visitor at the Lazarus household. Lazarus and Steinthal, who was living with Lazarus, were thinking of publishing a magazine to be called *Zeitschrift für Völkerpsychologie und Sprachwissenschaft*. Dilthey spent long hours with them discussing the problems of a basic science of human affairs and the contributions which the social psychology movement had made to it.[45]

This movement was a continuation of the ideas of Wilhelm von Humboldt and the philosopher and psychologist Johann Friedrich Herbart. It started from the Herbartian dictum that man is what society makes him. It believed that ideas grow in time out of human experience in society, and in turn tend always to find expression, and thus to influence future human experience.[46] The drive to action comes from the individual mind, but the actual patterns of that action are always determined by the value patterns of the society in which the individual lives. Despite differ-

---

[44] *Ibid.*, pp. 7-8.   [45] *Der junge Dilthey*, p. 49.
[46] Moritz Lazarus, "Über den Ursprung der Sitten," *Zeitschrift für Völkerpsychologie und Sprachwissenschaft*, I (1860), 408, 459.

ences between societies a universal standard of ethical action arises in the universal psychological nature of the individual, and patterns of a universal ethics develop out of the individual mind in a teleological manner.[47]

Ideas build the essence of history, the *Völkerpsychologie* movement argued. Out of the interactions of individuals in society there grows not only an individual mind and ideas but also a community mind.[48] This community is objectified in language, tools and machines, symbols, institutions, ideas, values, and feelings.[49] These are called collectively the objective mind. Lazarus and Steinthal agreed with Humboldt that ideas themselves never exist independently of individuals.[50] They are important only insofar as they are comprehended and put into action by individuals. The process of history is thus the realization of ideas. "How rich might man be," Lazarus mused, "if he consciously promoted the ideas which have grown up in his midst out of the teleological nature of the human mind." [51]

This movement, as a whole, emphasized a "scientific psychology" (a purely honorific term) as opposed to the metaphysical psychology which had been dominant under Hegel's influence. Lazarus and Steinthal thus offered a middle ground between history and the natural sciences. History was interested in the realm of the unique, the spirit, and of change; natural science in the consistent, in the process of the formation of laws. Psychology was to be a bridge between history and natural science because it dealt

---

[47] *Ibid.*, pp. 464-66, 469.

[48] Moritz Lazarus, "Einige synthetische Gedanken zur Völkerpsychologie," *Zeitschrift für Völkerpsychologie und Sprachwissenschaft,* (1865), 111.

[49] *Ibid.*, p. 53.

[50] Moritz Lazarus, "Über die Ideen in der Geschichte," *Zeitschrift für Völkerpsychologie und Sprachwissenschaft,* III (1865), 425.

[51] *Ibid.*, p. 485.

with the spirit and historical actions in an attempt to form natural laws. In combining the advantages of both methods Lazarus and Steinthal hoped to penetrate more closely social and cultural reality.

To carry on his frequent debates with Lazarus and Steinthal on the nature of the human studies and of historical reality, Dilthey began an intensive study of Humboldt and Herbart. When Dilthey learned (in 1860) that Lazarus was leaving Berlin to take a professorship at Bern, he wrote to his parents: "I am grateful to Lazarus for inspiring the development of my ideas." [52]

A brief glance at Dilthey's position with regard to the *Völkerpsychologie* movement, which could be called a determined attempt to bridge the gap between positivism and historicism, will indicate clearly his attitude toward the two movements. There were, to be sure, positivistic leanings in Dilthey's own views. He felt that the historical school erred in rejecting the psychological foundations of the human sciences which Lazarus had tried to build up; he also believed that the search for laws of human behavior was a valid quest.[53]

In general, Dilthey overwhelmingly rejected the fundamental positivistic assumptions and methodology of *Völkerpsychologie*. He argued that the laws to be found in human social behavior were not natural laws and that psychology, which should help create a foundation for the human sciences, could not be a positivistic psychology.[54] The twenty-five year old Dilthey entered into many heated debates with Lazarus on the extent to which the methods of the natural sciences could be assimilated into the human

[52] *Der junge Dilthey,* p. 128.
[53] Dilthey, *Gesammelte Schriften,* V, 27; also *Der junge Dilthey,* pp. 140-41.
[54] *Der junge Dilthey,* p. 49.

sciences. "I have at least caused him to doubt the limits
of the movement and the terms he uses," commented Dilthey to his brother.[55] During the 1860s Dilthey attempted
to put down his specific objections to the Lazarus-Steinthal
movement and to positivism in general as a methodology
for the human sciences in an article called "Contra Laza-
rism et Lazaristas, Millium etc." [56] This article that was
never published furnished the foundation for his first published systematic work, *Introduction to the Science of
Man*.[57]

Those elements of the *Völkerpsychologie* movement of
which Dilthey approved were clearly those which traced
their origins to historicism. The concept of the unfolding
of ideas from the drives of the individual and their fulfillment in expressions which were called collectively the objective mind was a basic aspect of the historical approach.
Ideas working through finite individuals strove for universality and fulfillment in history, and a program of ethical
action was to be founded upon the promotion of those
ideas which grew up in history.

Dilthey further developed his ideas about historical reality and the nature of a science of human activities in lively
debates in the meetings of the "Suicide Club," which he
frequented after receiving his licentiate in 1864.[58] During
these discussions there were sharp conflicts concerning the
crisis of historicism. The tradition of the German movement was most strongly defended by Hermann Grimm, the
son of Wilhelm and nephew of Jakob Grimm. Hermann
Grimm was a determined and eloquent defender of the doc-

[55] *Ibid.*, p. 51.
[56] *Ibid.*, p. 142.
[57] Dilthey, *Einleitung in die Geisteswissenschaften* (Berlin, 1883).
[58] Bernhard Erdmannsdorfer, "Alfred Boretius," *Preussische Jahrbücher*, CIV (1904), 5-6.

trine of the influence of great men in history against the democratizing inroads of positivism into the human sciences. Grimm, for example, did not try to understand Goethe in relation to the state, science, politics, or philosophy of Goethe's age, but only to understand his poetry, the life experience of Goethe himself.[59] In stressing the importance of personality in history, and of the life of the individual reflected in his inner experience as a key to personality, Grimm was fully backed by Dilthey, then steeped in the study of Schleiermacher.

The main champion of the positivistic trend was Wilhelm Scherer, the brilliant young Austrian philologian. Scherer was one of the important figures in German literature of the nineteenth century. Following the example of Mill and Buckle, he tried to show that speech and literature were parts of an endless chain of cause and effect. He attempted to endow the human sciences with the same sureness of method that the natural sciences enjoyed. He sought for the natural historical laws of genesis in literature and built a comprehensive history of German literature around these principles.[60] Despite his enthusiasm for positivism almost to the exclusion of other points of view, he remained one of Dilthey's closest friends throughout his life.

In the debates of the Suicide Club the positivistic and historicist point of view came into sharp but illuminating conflict. Dilthey, in his memorial essay on Scherer, indicated the topics covered. These seem to be a review of Dilthey's own interests.

[59] Cf. Dilthey's review of Hermann Grimm, *Goethe: Vorlesungen* (2 vols.; Berlin, 1877), in Wilhelm Dilthey, "Über die Einbildungskraft der Dichter," *Zeitschrift für Völkerpsychologie und Sprachwissenschaft*, X (1878), 42-104.

[60] Dilthey, "Wilhelm Scherer zu persönlichem Gedächtnis" (1886), in *Gesammelte Schriften*, XI, 236-53.

The political influence created by the strivings of our people
for national unity gave our study of literature a practical aspect. The investigation of the works of the romantics, especially Friedrich Schlegel and Novalis, aroused more free and
more German discussions concerning the nature of historical
continuity than had Mill, Comte and Buckle. An investigation of the influence of history's great men initiated by Carlyle, Emerson and Ranke taught us to regard them differently
than did English and French writers. From the concept of
the life ideal, developed best by Schleiermacher, we gained
a well-grounded insight into poetry and its unfolding of national life.[61]

Dilthey reacted to the challenge of positivism not only
by reaffirming the basic ideals and practices of historicism
but also by arguing that these had to be revised and extended in two ways. In order to meet the need of a
stronger foundation for the historicist position, he argued
that a critique of historical reason was needed to complete
the work of the historical school. Moreover, in order to
bring history into closer contact with life, historians must
take the lead in the political education of the nation.

The importance of a scientific foundation for the historical and human sciences was illustrated by Dilthey's own
point of view. Later in his life, when he was analyzing the
growth of the "natural systems" in the Renaissance period,
Dilthey outlined the typical development of a new world
outlook.[62] He sketched the pattern of development in four
stages. In the beginning a new outlook grew primarily out
of a new life-relationship which no longer fitted within the
old categories. The new life-relationship then expressed
itself in new concepts and in fragmentary systems in poetry

---

[61] *Ibid.,* XI, 243.

[62] Dilthey, "Der entwicklungsgeschichtliche Pantheismus" (1900), in
Gesammelte Schriften, II, 312-14.

and unsystematized thought. Out of the early studies there grew up comprehensive, systematic metaphysical constructions. Finally, the new world-view reached maturity when critical investigations laid the epistemological bases for these systems. Only in this final stage, said Dilthey, could lasting progress be made toward understanding the phenomena of historical reality.

Seen in the light of this typology, the historical school had constructed partial systems and had given inspiration to metaphysical systematic constructions, but until Dilthey's time they still lacked the epistemological foundation for their work. In Dilthey's view they had set to work empirically without a critical understanding of what they were doing or a knowledge of the exact nature of the objects with which they were dealing.[63] They therefore left their work in separate compartments and failed to make their studies into a science of human affairs. Their most advanced representatives, Boeckh and Ranke, had done a tremendous amount of empirical investigation and had developed intensive and successful techniques for the investigation of the past. They had been entered, to a limited extent, upon a discussion of their methods. But they could not be called universal philosophical students of the human sciences. The only attempt at a systematic and comprehensive view of the human sciences had been undertaken by thinkers who started from other assumptions than those of the human sciences. The idealist philosopher Hegel started from a metaphysical viewpoint; the positivist philosophers Comte and Spencer started from a naturalistic viewpoint. To Dilthey their systems were all metaphysical constructions, not critical systems.

[63] Dilthey, "Einleitung in die Geisteswissenschaften" (1883), in *Gesammelte Schriften,* I, 49.

As early as 1859 Dilthey felt compelled to step in and furnish the tremendous amount of empirical study, which the historical school had brought forth, with a critical foundation which would grow out of the material itself rather than out of the natural sciences. In this way he hoped to resolve the conflict between the historical school, the abstract theorists, and the positivists. He sought to grasp the expressions of the historical world in all their multiplicity. As Kant had built a critique of pure reason, Dilthey would construct a critique of historical reason. The foundation would be found in the nature of the historical human being.

The function of the historian, Dilthey felt, was to help in this endeavor. Too long had the historian been content with fragmentary studies. Now was the time for the historian to investigate critically the assumptions upon which they worked and to build their empirical findings into a generalized science of human cultural behavior.

But closely connected with this theoretical task, according to Dilthey's early views, there was an educational task. Historians, he said, stand in immediate relationship to political life and understand it as do no other type of intellectual.[64] It was therefore the duty of the historian to lead the way in the formation of public policy through the education of public opinion. The historian was the ideal type of man; he had his foundations in both the problems of the present and in the stream of culture which gives the present meaning. The historian understood historical reason, the thought patterns which grew up empirically as a result of human actions. The historian appreciated how one generation thus prepared the way for the next and how that

[64] Dilthey, "Johannes von Müller" (1865), in *Gesammelte Schriften,* XI, 79.

generation carried on the tradition of the earlier generations.[65] The historian best perceived how values evolved
over a period of years and how the most intelligent policy
was to follow the development of those values, adding to
them and adapting them to the new situations rather than
making breaks in the evolution.

Consequently, it was the duty of the historian to use his
knowledge to promote social and political progress in accordance with historical development and thus to serve
life. It was the duty of the historian to keep the community of human values alive and to defend them against all
revolutionary attempts on the part of the state to substitute
political values for them.

German idealism was the second of the intellectual
movements to mold Dilthey's thought in the 1860s. The
attraction of idealism for Dilthey was that this view filled
in and rounded out the outlines of the pantheism which he
had developed as a youth. Having started in this tradition
and grown up in it, Dilthey never left it. It was the pantheistic view, matured into a realistic teleological idealism,
against which all other views were measured and to which
Dilthey periodically returned for fresh inspiration.

This view was idealistic because it regarded ultimate
reality to be of the same nature as the human mind. It was
teleological because it argued that not only was the reality
of the individual to be found in the idea which gave it form
but that the pattern of its growth was also determined by
that innate idea. It was realistic because it believed that
ideas could be known as they were in reality through the
instrumentality of the human mind.

Dilthey had come into contact with the idealist tradition

[65] *Der junge Dilthey,* p. 190.

early in life.[66] At Heidelberg he had been turned to philosophy by Kuno Fischer, whose studies of German idealism did much to bring about a revival of idealism in the 1860s. Then, at Berlin, Dilthey's investigation of the history of ideas in the Middle Ages led him to an intensive study of Hegel. He began for the first time to work out a systematic approach to the study of ideas in history on a basis of Hegelian methodology in April and May of 1860.[67]

Dilthey was attracted to idealism as a result of his investigations of Schleiermacher's philosophy, both in connection with the edition of his letters and under the guidance of his philosophical mentor, Adolf Trendelenburg. The work on Schleiermacher's letters led Dilthey into a thorough investigation of the early stages of German idealism in order to understand more clearly Schleiermacher's views.[68] Later on when he was writing a life of Schleiermacher, the idealists again demanded even more consideration than the immediate study of the hero himself.[69] Schleiermacher was also the subject of several essays written under Trendelenburg's guidance for the degree. In January, 1864, he published his dissertation, *On the Principles of Schleiermacher's Ethics*,[70] and was granted the doctorate after having publicly defended the dissertation.

The foundations of a realistic teleological idealism were to be discovered in the age of the German movement as were the bases of historicism. The starting point was Kant's philosophy, which was based upon the assumption that the process of how we come to know is the main problem of philosophy, and that a critical method must be de-

---

[66] See Chapter I for complete discussion.
[67] *Der junge Dilthey*, pp. 121, 124.
[68] *Ibid.*, pp. 67, 110, 137, 159.   [69] *Ibid.*, p. 208.
[70] Wilhelm Dilthey, *De Principiis ethicis Schleiermacheri* (Berlin, 1864).

veloped which would distinguish between the area of certain knowledge and of hypothetical speculation. Kant's critical method defined and determined the form of Dilthey's thought. Kant, in his *Critique of Pure Reason,* argued that the only knowledge that can be known for certain is phenomenal knowledge, the knowledge about the world which we receive through the senses. Our knowledge of this outer world is not an exact reflection of it, for the unity which we see in this world is something given it by the forms of the mind, first of all by the *a priori* forms of the intuitions—of space and time—and then by the schemata and the categories of the understanding—such as quantity, quality, relation, and modality. In so giving form to the outer world, we make it intelligible to the human mind. We then can never know the world of "things-in-themselves," which exist beyond the categories of time and space. In Kant's doctrine of the world of phenomena, his attempted creation of a realistic idealism is apparent. The forms of knowledge come from the mind and constitute the idealistic element. But the assumption that the material of thought is given from without is a realistic one.

After having denied the stamp of approval of scientific knowledge to the metaphysical world, Kant then proceeded to rebuild metaphysics in a subjective, idealistic manner. Ideas such as God, immortality, and freedom can never be scientifically proven or disproven. They are the conditions of the moral life, and their reality must be believed in, said Kant. These ideas grow out of the practical needs of the mind to fulfill itself in conceptualization and expression. Several minds interacting upon one another then clarify concepts of this sort. Since the concepts are expressions of the mind, the history of man's ideas is thus the working out of the potentialities of the human mind into actual expres-

sion. Each generation of minds works out this nature a
little more fully. This general teleological view, inade-
quately explained by Kant, was made by Hegel into the
foundation of his system.

Hegel attempted to reconcile the mind and nature, subject and object, ideal and real, which Kant had brought
into contact but not into harmony, into different phases of
one essence. In doing this he reconstructed upon a more
critical basis the pantheistic views of the romantic philosopher Friedrich von Schelling. The latter had taught the
interpermeation of nature and spirit in a dialectical and
evolutionary pattern which came very close to Dilthey's
own ideas of an evolutionary pantheism. Hegel said that
phenomena are both subjectively and objectively real because nature and spirit were both expressions of an Absolute Mind unfolding itself in history.

According to Hegel both the outer world and man himself were in a continual process of development of the potentialities of man's mind or reason. In fact, the end and
immanent purpose of history was the realization of man's
full potentialities. Not only did reason triumph in the life
of both the individual and society but the world itself was
shown to be reason in the process of development in a dialectical process.[71] With the identity of the subject and the
object as rationality, the tension between the individual
and the world was dissolved and both could be free. Absolute freedom and absolute knowledge could be attained;
they were, in fact, identical.[72] Here historicism and idealism met and were fused into one system.

In Schleiermacher's thought, man strives to see more of

[71] Georg Wilhelm Friedrich Hegel, *Hegel's Philosophy of Right,* trans.
and ed. by T. M. Knox (Oxford, 1942), p. 10. (Note that the title of
Hegel's book reads, *Grundlinien der Philosophie des Rechts.*)
[72] *Ibid.,* p. 222.

the universal in the particular, and more of the particular in the universal. He strives to make the ideal more and more real, and the real more and more ideal. He strives to have everything in time and space full of meaning, and to give everything meaningful a local habitation and a name. Coupled with this human striving is a belief in its connection with reality, a conviction that the ground or basis for ideal experience already exists, that man is not seeking a mirage, but the actual, a reality as yet known only in part.[73] In Schleiermacher's system, realism and idealism were most easily reconciled. It was for this reason that Dilthey was so strongly drawn to him.

In the midst of contending philosophical parties, Trendelenburg attempted to establish knowledge upon a solid foundation which could be accepted by all. In so doing he reconstructed a realistic idealism which was based on Aristotle's doctrine that the forms of knowledge are at the same time both forms of thought and forms of reality.[74] Trendelenburg declared that the laws of logic were based upon both subjective thought and objective reality. In founding them genetically in subjective thinking he made logic a part of psychology and epistemology, and thus more than a study of mere formulas of thinking. He described the logical processes as they grew from the simple mental operation to the more complex. In the Aristotelian manner he built up the logical structure of induction and deduction from the psychological foundations of sense, memory and experience. For Trendelenburg there was no pure thought but only experience working in man.[75] The thought of the

[73] *Schleiermacher's Soliloquies,* trans. by Horace Leland Friess (Chicago, 1926), pp. 140-41.
[74] Adolf Trendelenburg, *Logische Untersuchungen* (2 vols.; Leipzig, 1870), I, ix.
[75] *Ibid.,* I, 331.

individual being was thus only the accumulation of his reflection upon his experiences and furnished the ideal unity
of that experience. For Trendelenburg, truth always grew
up in the mind of the individual. The sum total of each
individual's thought made up the thought of the race. The
history of philosophy was the history of man's reflection
upon his experiences.

Because of his basically historical manner of regarding
man's knowledge of reality, Trendelenburg has often been
called the logician of the historical school. Trendelenburg
regarded, as did Dilthey, the problem of understanding and
the problem of reconstructive action as complementary aspects of human thought and activity. His theory of understanding and logic was complemented by a theory of ethics
and social action.

In the process of knowledge there is a continual interaction between existence and thought. Things not only determine thoughts but thoughts to some degree also determine the things which they portray, asserted Trendelenburg.[76] Thus, in any scientific theory, there is always an
element of thought and an element of being, of subjectivity
and objectivity. From this point of view, "the real is sub-
ordinate, logically and in fact, to the ideal; and the ideal is
teleologically realized in the real." He further stated:
"The philosophy which seeks to demonstrate and to develop this view dispenses with the equivocal identity of the
subjective and the objective but unites and harmonizes
realism and idealisms."[77] Because reality partakes of both
mind and being, mind can come to know reality.

Trendelenburg's theory of ethical action was very closely
related to his theories of knowledge and logic. In his

[76] *Ibid.*, p. 331.
[77] *Ibid.*, p. 538.

"Natural Law on the Basis of Ethics" Trendelenburg set forth his fundamental principles of ethics and law.[78] In agreement with Aristotle and in contradiction to modern theory, Trendelenburg did not separate the moral and the legal aspects of man's social life. In both cases the basic outlines evolved in a teleological fashion from the nature of man.[79] Man was capable of thinking of himself in relation to the universal forms or principles. Thinking in universal terms in this manner was ethical thinking, according to Trendelenburg. Thus man in realizing his own form or idea, his own reality, was performing an ethical act.[80] The ethical problem was the "realization of man as man." [81]

Ethics were based upon the action of every individual, said Trendelenburg. In man many partial ends sought realization at once. In order for the individual to live an ethical life, the universal or ethical end had to control these partial ends.[82] That control was effected through the will. Trendelenburg defined will as "desire permeated by thought." The ability of the will to set for itself universal aims and ends rather than merely the fulfillment of sensual desires Trendelenburg termed the freedom of the will. Such freedom, he said, is not innate but is acquired only in the course of man's development.[83]

The ethical realization of the teleological idea of man was to take place only in a community, said Trendelenburg.[84] Law, stated Trendelenburg, is the complex of those universal rules of action within which the ethical

[78] Friedrich Adolf Trendelenburg, *Naturrecht auf dem Grunde der Ethik* (Leipzig, 1868).

[79] *Ibid.,* p. 22.

[80] Trendelenburg, *Logische Untersuchungen,* II, 106.

[81] Trendelenburg, *Naturrecht auf dem Grunde der Ethik,* p. 94.

[82] Trendelenburg, *Logische Untersuchungen,* II, 107.

[83] *Ibid.,* p. 112.

[84] Trendelenburg, *Naturrecht auf dem Grunde der Ethik,* p. 41.

community and its members could be preserved and developed.[85] Legal right guards the external conditions necessary for the realization of ethical requirements within the confines of the state. In fact, the idea of the state was "to realize universal man in the individual form and in the nation." [86] Man develops his nature only in the state and in history. The character of man and its growing realization in time was the moving spring of the world's history. The ethical aim of human action in history was to further develop the nature of man toward the fulfillment of his potentialities.

As with the crisis in historicism so also in the crisis of German idealism, Dilthey attempted to resolve the latter crisis by a reexamining and reconstructing of the original foundations. This was most clearly brought out in his evaluation of Kant's solution to the epistemological question.

Kant's philosophy was for Dilthey, as for most of the philosophers of the nineteenth century, a vast mine of ideas and conceptual tools which were to be used in full or in part, altered or disregarded, as the user saw fit. Perhaps more than most other philosophers, Dilthey emphasized in the 1860s the importance of a critical foundation in the Kantian manner for knowledge in the historically oriented human sciences. Such a critique would round out and unify on a scientific basis the work of the historical school. "Our task is clearly marked for us," he said in his inaugural address at Basel in 1867, "to follow Kant's critical path to the end and to establish an empirical science of the human mind in collaboration with workers in other fields." [87]

Dilthey followed Kant then in saying that the starting point of any investigation of the nature of knowledge and

85 *Ibid.*, p. 71.   86 *Ibid.*, p. 92.
87 Dilthey, *Gesammelte Schriften*, V, 27.

of man must be in the way in which experience becomes knowledge in the mind. He agreed with Kant that metaphysical assumptions as to the nature of the universe and reality were outmoded foundations for a philosophy.[88]

Although he accepted Kant's major proposition and set as his main aim the creation of a critique of historical reason, Dilthey declined to follow Kant much further. First of all, he protested that both Kant and the positivists had been too intellectual in dealing with the process of knowledge in "pure" terms and had thus neglected the real nature of man. Cognition, Dilthey insisted, cannot be explained by itself but only as a part of an integral human consciousness which wills and feels as well as it reasons.[89] Dilthey also argued that Kant did not deal adequately with the influence of historical and social conditions upon thought.[90] In the historical and Aristotelian tradition, Dilthey argued that ideas grew out of history as well as out of reason. Finally, Dilthey pointed out that the critical method should not be limited to the natural sciences alone, as the Neo-Kantians had done, but that it had also to be extended to the human, historical sciences. Universal and necessary knowledge of other human minds was knowledge of reality, not just phenomena. Whereas the scientist dealt with the external world, the historian dealt with thoughts, feelings, and actions he could experience by a process of reliving.

To Dilthey Hegel seemed to have moved two steps further toward the solution of the epistemological problem. Hegel had not only considered reason to have a foundation in historical process as well as in the mind, but also the realm of ethics and law—as well as art, religion, and phi-

[88] *Der junge Dilthey,* p. 153.
[89] Dilthey, "Einleitung in die Geisteswissenschaften," in *Gesammelte Schriften,* I, xviii.
[90] *Der junge Dilthey,* p. 151.

losophy—were brought within the critical framework. Hegel undoubtedly also attracted Dilthey because his concept of a dynamic reason which pervaded man's creations in history might be regarded as a secularization of Dilthey's own formulation of an evolutionary pantheism which realized itself in even higher forms.

However, there was still one major point, which caused Dilthey to reject Hegel as a guide for the construction of a critique of historical reason. Hegel, along with Kant, had created a purely intellectual and metaphysical pattern. He thus did injustice, said Dilthey, to man's essentially irrational nature.[91]   But in Schleiermacher, Dilthey found more emphasis on the irrational elements in the process of cognition and on the historical nature of human reason as expressed in man's institutions and culture. (Schleiermacher, however, remained a Kantian in his agnosticism with respect to absolute substance, asserting that knowledge reveals only a manifold of interrelated phenomena.[92]

It was Trendelenburg more than Schleiermacher who supplied Dilthey with specific arguments for the possibility of historical knowledge. According to both Trendelenburg and Dilthey, the common ground of man's inner experience acted as the connecting link between the inner ideas, which were science, and the outer cultural and institutional expressions of man, which were historical reality.

Later in life Dilthey developed further his concept of world-views, which drew their inspiration directly from Trendelenburg's typology. Dilthey tended to share with Trendelenburg the middle position of an objective and teleological idealism in which thought and force, mind and matter, interacted and interpenetrated. Dilthey was too

---

[91] Dilthey, *Gesammelte Schriften*, I, 87-89.
[92] Schleiermacher's *Soliloquies*, p. 126.

much of a realist and an empiricist to accept the complete domination of the mind over the flux of history. Yet, unless mind and matter interacted, there was no possibility of the influence of the intellect and of ideas in the world.

On his seventieth birthday Dilthey reminisced that "no one can imagine his (Trendelenburg's) power. It lay in the fashion in which he made the individual investigation into history as a whole" and showed each philosophical system as a part of the realization of man's nature.[93] Trendelenburg embodied the conviction that the history of philosophy was to be studied in its continuity in order to lay the foundation for the conception of the ideal unity of all things.

In answer, then, to the challenge of idealism by naturalism, Dilthey remained wholly, although critically, within the traditional camp. He emphasized, that idealism would have to be founded upon a more realistic basis if it were to overcome the crisis brought on by the challenge to the truths it held to be self-evident. It would have to recognize both the historical and the emotional and volitional nature of cognition as complementary to the accepted critical view. Moreover, if it were to be effective as a social and scientific force it would have to extend the critical foundations beyond the natural sciences and to include also the historically orientated sciences within the realm of a critically founded science. A critique of historical reason was to be the solution for the crisis of idealism, as well as for the crisis of historicism. It would solve the crisis of science in general.

[93] Dilthey, *Gesammelte Schriften*, V, 7-8.

III

THE HISTORICAL

WORLD

Dilthey strove to distinguish the human sciences from the natural sciences. This distinction was his methodological starting point. If the methods of the natural sciences could have been incorporated into the realm of the human sciences, the conflict between the two methodologies would not have arisen. As early as 1859 Dilthey had distinguished between a "system of laws or sciences" and a "system of significant and value-permeated existence," or world-views.[1]

The problems of the human sciences as understood by Dilthey can, therefore, best be understood by contrasting them with the natural sciences. The natural sciences for Dilthey dealt with the nonhuman world. They dealt with phenomena as abstracted series of relations. For this reason the natural sciences could take phenomena out of context, substitute symbols for them, and mathematically manipulate those symbols to create algebraic laws of phenomenal behavior. These algebraic laws were then known as natural scientific laws. In this sense the natural sciences built up a structure of knowledge tested by experimental repetition which it called "science." Dilthey, however, believed that the human sciences dealt with a human world, the product of an active mind with free will; they studied and interpreted phenomena as expressions of an

---

[1] Quoted by Georg Misch in his "Einleitung" (Introduction) to Vol. V of Dilthey, *Gesammelte Schriften*, p. xx.

inner spiritual reality. The human sciences could not remove phenomena from their historical context, as it was the context which gave them meaning. They had to be studied in their historical setting as part of the pattern of meaning and value which they formed. Human science led to a creation not of laws, but of systems of values. In this manner the human sciences built up a structure of knowledge based on corroborative evidence, which Dilthey called a "world-view." [2]

Having defined his field as that of the historical human sciences regarded philosophically, Dilthey had to determine the exact nature of the historical world before he could build a critique of historical reason. Unless the historical world was accessible to human understanding, there could be no true historical knowledge. In addition, the nature of the historical world would determine the manner in which it could be known. Could it be known directly and intimately, or must one assume in the historical world, as Kant had done in the physical world, that one could never know the reality of things in themselves?

In order to gain a philosophical understanding of the development of one aspect of thought, Dilthey studied the philosophers and poets who seemed to offer a key to that development. Certain poets and philosophers reflected his own view that there was a unifying spirit permeating nature and running through history. They presented a unified world-view in which the aim of understanding life, out of life itself, complemented an historical interest in the products of the creative human mind. Such life philosophies appeared recurrently throughout the history of Western civilization (e.g., the Stoics, Giordano Bruno, Baruch Spinoza, Goethe, Wilhelm von Humboldt, Friedrich

[2] *Ibid.,* p. xix.

Schlegel, Schleiermacher).[3]　Dilthey looked upon these thinkers as the creators of a great tradition in which the nature of man and his creations was always the center of investigation.

Life philosophies, said Dilthey, developed in times of rapid or profound social and ideological changes, when old systems were disintegrating. The new life philosophy marked the end of the old system of philosophy.[4] The breakdown of the natural systems of the Enlightenment fostered the growth of the pantheistic life philosophies of Goethe, Friedrich Schlegel, and Schleiermacher. Dilthey studied and learned from them all. In their thoughts Dilthey found a complex of three interconnected ideas which offered him an insight into the nature of the historical process. These ideas were those of a life philosophy, an evolutionary pantheism, and an historical relativism.

The philosophical starting point of this tradition and of Dilthey's own system was a man's active life. From a study of the great poets of the tradition—Shakespeare, Cervantes, and Goethe—arose "the ruling impulse of [Dilthey's] philosophical thinking, the desire to understand life out of a study of life itself." [5]　For Dilthey the human world was the matrix of all reality. "All thought goes back to life and behind life one cannot go." [6]　As in Trendelenburg's teleological idealism, so too in Dilthey's thought, life and science, activity and contemplation, were bound up in an inseparable whole. That which was to be studied was the structural complex which was both action and thought together. In Trendelenburg's sense, reality was

---

[3] *Der junge Dilthey,* p. 197.
[4] *Gesammelte Schriften,* II, 51, 253, 287, 290.
[5] Dilthey, "Vorrede," in *Gesammelte Schriften,* V, 4.
[6] *Ibid.,* p. 3.

the process of interaction between them. This philosophy Dilthey called a life philosophy. It was a secularization of the pantheistic notion of the union of the world and the spirit.

The continued interaction of the thought and the action of all the individuals of a society formed a great life stream in which human potentialities were realized. This life stream could be studied only in the various artistic expressions and philosophical systems of man.[7] Each moment in the life stream of society was connected closely with every other moment in that stream. Each generation works for and realizes the fulfillment of its capabilities in the following generations.[8] This was the teleological process of history.

For Dilthey the study of life and of history became almost identical. "History is only life, comprehended from the point of view of all mankind, built into a unity." [9] Not only did history give a wider scope to the study of different possible life situations, but the present situation was made what is was by the fact that it was built upon history, upon past life situations. The essence of the historical world was the continuous interaction of human minds with their environment in time and space. This uninterrupted process Dilthey called the "universal-historical continuum." [10]

This uninterrupted interaction of life and thought in the "universal-historical continuum" was the basis for the evolutionary pantheism of the life philosopher. By evolutionary pantheism Dilthey meant the gradual realization in the world of phenomena of forms imparted by a universal im-

[7] Misch, "Einleitung," p. xxxvi.
[8] *Der junge Dilthey,* p. 190.
[9] Dilthey, *Gesammelte Schriften,* VII, 256.
[10] Misch, "Einleitung," p. xv.

manent idea or spirit. Dilthey viewed history as a vast life
stream out of which immanent forms were realized and expressed in a teleological fashion in the objective creations
of the human mind. History was immanent in all life expressions, be they artifacts, social institutions, or value systems. Here, too, will be recognized the secularization of
the pantheistic views of Dilthey's early years. The idea
was best expressed in Goethe's concept of a pantheistic
stream of historical being which acted as the unifying and
form-giving force of human society.[11]

Dilthey's study of each of the recurrences of an evolutionary pantheism contributed to his own understanding of
the historical world. It was Stoicism that first secularized
pantheism into the idea of the *logos,* the universal reason
pervading history. Dilthey received from Stoicism his introduction to the understanding of universal history.[12]
The Stoic view was further developed in the evolutionary
pantheism of Nicolaus Cusanus and Giordano Bruno.
Permeated by the historical consciousness of the Renaissance, they developed a system in which man progressively
unfolded an immanent God-spirit in history.[13] In the philosophy of the classical German age, Spinoza's pantheism
was given more explicit and definite expression in the philological and literary studies of the romantics. The partial
systems of Wilhelm von Humboldt, Friedrich Schlegel, and
Schleiermacher culminated in the historical dialectic of
Hegel, in the historical consciousness of Ranke, and above
all, in the universal view of history of Friedrich Schlosser.

Schlosser viewed universal history as a kind of theodicy
of mankind in which man was evolving in a teleological

[11] *Der junge Dilthey,* 142; "Goethe," in *Das Erlebnis und die Dichtung.* Dilthey cites such works of Goethe as *Faust,* Part I, *Werther,*
and *Prometheus.*
[12] Misch, "Einleitung," p. xli.   [13] *Ibid.*

manner toward a realization of his potentialities, toward a rational world view.[14] The key to history lay in the gulf which existed between the ideal man of the human race and individual living men.[15] Literature, the arts, religion, and the state, were all imperfect expressions of the universal moral nature in man. As history evolved, more and more of that moral nature was realized. The potentialities of man's rational nature thus existed in a pantheistic and teleological fashion throughout all history, determined history's goals and values, and in their realization unified the stream of culture. In the writings of Schlosser the ideal of an evolutionary pantheism reached its height. Dilthey's own thoughts reflected Schlosser's view.

The union of the life-philosophy and the evolutionary pantheism was the basis of Dilthey's view of the historical process. Man, by nature, had to express himself. Those expressions that were recorded, formed the universal historical stream. This stream became man's cultural environment, and it helped to shape his further thoughts. Life expression thus not only determined the future course of history, but was in turn molded by the past course of history. Man engaged, then, in a continual process of taking from the stream of history, refining the contents in terms of his own interests, and giving the refined product back to the stream. In the process he developed his own nature more fully; he also gradually moved history in the direction of the realization of his own nature. History was thus slowly evolving toward a self-realization.

Out of this historical process evolved the true history of ideas. Ideas were the expression of the universal mind of man in contact with life. Every idea which man created

[14] Dilthey, "F. C. Schlosser" (1862), in *Gesammelte Schriften*, IX, 139.
[15] *Ibid.*, p. 141.

in history was conditioned both by the teleological manner in which universal human nature was realized, and by the life situation out of which it grew. Every idea was limited and, at the same time, given meaning by its place in the universal-historical continuum. Because ideas were thus a reflection of both the eternal nature of man and of the life situation in history, they were the key to the understanding of the historical world. As an expression of the interaction of mind and environment throughout history, the universal history of ideas furnished the dynamic structural unity of universal life. The universal history of ideas was the cement of the historical world; it furnished the empirical foundation for a critique of historical reason.

From his historical study Dilthey became aware of the limited nature of every historical occurrence, be it religion, an ideal, or a philosophic system. In the Rankean manner he regarded every age as immediate to God. The value of any age was true for that age but could not with validity be applied to other ages. For Dilthey historical relativism did not imply pessimism. On the contrary, it made man aware of his place in history, and thus it enhanced his rank as participant in the unfolding of the historical consciousness. The end of history was the historical movement itself, rather than a posited goal.[16] By historical movement Dilthey meant "the working of one generation for the following." [17] Man, determined by history, expressed in it his creative actions, thus creating new values. These values, then, became the norm for the succeeding generation, which in turn, created new values. This historical conditioning of value systems was important for an understanding of all philosophy, for man came to reality only in history. "The historical world-view is the emancipation of

---

[16] *Der junge Dilthey*, p. 191.   [17] *Ibid.*, p. 90.

the human mind from the last chain which science and philosophy have not yet broken." [18]

The specific problem of the critique of historical reason was, therefore, to understand the manner in which the human mind came to know the stream of history. Dilthey found the empirical methods for gaining a knowledge of the historical world in aesthetic, in philosophical, and philological criticism. His task was to organize a general philosophical justification for what the critics had been doing empirically, as Kant had philosophically justified the methods of the natural scientists in the realm of the mathematical and physical sciences.

There were three methods by which Dilthey analyzed the process of how one came to know the world of human studies. First of all, in the manner of Hegel and Ranke, he looked at the problem of history from the point of view of understanding the historical stream itself and the ideas represented in it. Secondly, following Schleiermacher's method of hermeneutics, Dilthey tried to understand the way in which the universal ideas of the historical stream came to be in an individual. Finally, from a study of the Kantian categories and Trendelenburg's types, he attempted to establish the forms in which historical reason was formulated in the human mind. (The study of types was an attempt to answer the problems of historical relativism.) These three methods might be thought of as the counterparts of the three aspects of the nature of the historical process.

Hegel and Ranke had both assumed a universal stream of history, such as Dilthey had posited as the basis of historical reality. The key to the understanding of this historical stream, for Dilthey, was its becoming objectified in

[18] Dilthey, *Gesammelte Schriften*, V, 9.

symbols. The symbol was the objectifying of the life expressive universal-historical continuum. Paintings, books, buildings, tools, documents, letters were historical performances symbolic of the life stream of history. These symbolic creations were the only records with which the historian could deal, for they were the only immediate knowable part of the historical world. "All records show only the apparent forms of the truly existing inner reality," Dilthey asserted.[19]

Following Ranke, who had become famous for his intensive and dispassionate analysis of documents in an attempt to ascertain "what actually happened" in the past, Dilthey set forth the successive stages of historical understanding. Dilthey believed that by studying the symbolic expressions one could arrive at an understanding of the life situation behind them, and of the universal formative ideas of the life stream. By studying the symbolic expression of an individual, one could arrive at an understanding of the individual and his ideas. By studying the expressions of a generation, one could understand the generation and the ideas for which it stood. By studying the expression of universal history, one could understand universal history. Through an understanding of universal history, one could arrive at the structure and forms of the universal history of ideas. Thus, by a process of progressive analysis, one proceeded from the individual expression of the creative mind to an understanding of universal history of ideas.

Just as the spiritual always tended to express itself in symbol, so the symbol could perpetuate itself independent of the spirit which brought it forth. Devoid of its original creative meaning, the symbol's new meaning was imparted by the observer from his own frame of reference.[20] The

[19] *Der junge Dilthey,* p. 147.   [20] *Ibid.,* p. 147.

true historian, then, must not look at these symbols from the point of view of his own spiritual system, said Dilthey. He should try to grasp the spiritual system which gave rise to the symbols in order to understand them. The true historian must follow the development of ideas underneath the symbolic records which come to light, filling in the interstices between the symbols, reconstructing the flow of ideas.[21]

In striving to understand the universal historical stream of ideas, Dilthey followed Hegel's method of regarding every philosophical system as a step in the total development of philosophy. Dilthey made this method the foundation of what he called the "historical consciousness." This historical consciousness saw every historical performance as a reflection of the life of the time. "It seeks to make clear the intellectual atmosphere in which the writer creates. Although it uses philological findings, it regards these in connection with the atmosphere of the time, and shows in both the genesis of new ideas." [22] Historical method, for Dilthey, did not mean only a strictly philological criticism. "Historical method regarded the individual work as a link in the chain of the history of ideas, so that the stream of history rather than the individual works is the highest aim of investigation." [23]

The attempt to understand each work in an exact and scientific fashion, in relation to the stream of history, involved the study of hermeneutics. Although Dilthey regarded the comprehension of the universal historical stream as the final goal of historical understanding, he returned always to the individual symbolic work as the point of departure. An understanding of the individual work was possible, said Dilthey, only through trained intuitive in-

[21] *Ibid.,* p. 186.   [22] *Ibid.,* p. 150.   [23] *Ibid.,* p. 150.

sight. He disagreed strongly with the tendency in the early
1860s to echo Mill's belief that the method of the natural
sciences must be transposed to the human studies. The
processes of the natural world could be halted for purposes
of investigation and studied in laboratory conditions. This
was impossible with the historical stream, for only an intuitive insight could grasp the stream of a constantly chang-
ing history in its symbolic development.[24]

"Two streams of thought, which are of utmost importance for the history of intellectual movements, came to us
from the Kantian-Fichtean period," said Dilthey.[25] The
first of these two streams of thought, and the one most im-
mediately connected with the study of the universal stream
of ideas, was the axiom that "the individual is activity." [26]
Concurring with Fichte, Dilthey wrote in his diary that
"every thought is to be considered as a part of this activity.
Every system is to be explained out of the movement of
ideas; it is not to be taken as something finished." [27]

Dilthey agreed with Ranke and Humboldt that the starting point of the history of ideas was the creation of systems
of ideas by the interaction between the individual and the
stream of history.[28] Not only did the stream of history give
value to the individual, but the individual also imprinted
part of his own nature upon the creations and gave meaning and value to that stream.[29] This process of interaction
did not occur all at once. Dilthey agreed with Lessing that
systems of ideas did not spring full-bloomed into existence,
like Athena out of the head of Zeus, but grew up gradually
over a long period of time out of the interactions of many

[24] *Ibid.*, p. 190.   [25] *Ibid.*, p. 92.
[26] Wach, *Das Verstehen*, I, 248, III, 105.
[27] *Der junge Dilthey*, p. 93.
[28] Misch, "Einleitung," p. xv.
[29] Wach, *Das Verstehen*, I, 248, III, 105.

individuals in the stream of history.[30]   Incomplete ideas
grew into a system by a long process of interaction with
other fragmentary ideas which had also grown out of individuals in contact with their environment and with the
stream of history.   Systems of ideas grew up, became self-
realized, and took on a life of their own.   This self-realization of systems was the ultimate aim of the study of the
history of ideas.   The starting point always had to be the
acting philosopher, who realized his ideas in life.   Such a
philosopher was Schleiermacher, Dilthey believed.

For Schleiermacher, the universal experience of mankind was embodied in specific individuals.[31]   Like Fichte,
Schleiermacher made an understanding of the creative individual the starting point of his investigation.[32]   More
than any one else he had developed hermeneutics into a
technique of understanding other men and times through a
criticism of their literary productions.   In his work, the
developments of Biblical criticism since the 1760's, the
philological critical method as it was used by the historical
school, and the critical philosophy, were all for the first
time united into a common general method.[33]

Schleiermacher's procedure, of starting an investigation
of the symbolic work from an intensive analysis of the creative individual, became Dilthey's own pattern.   The individual was to be studied from himself.   The inner development of the individual's intellectual growth was the
exclusive theme of Schleiermacher's hermeneutics.[34]   "Paul
was understood from a study of Paul himself, not from a
study of Philo or Josephus," Dilthey emphasized.[35]   In

---

[30] *Der junge Dilthey*, p. 190.
[31] Dilthey, *Gesammelte Schriften*, V, 4.
[32] *Der junge Dilthey*, p. 87.
[33] *Ibid.*, p. 87.   [34] *Ibid.*, p. 91.   [35] *Ibid.*

order to understand how ideas grew, one had to follow the entire process of interaction in the individual from the beginning. One could not merely abstract common denominators. Such abstractions led only to a false system of construction.[36] The true historian was a fellow worker with the original artist. He had to follow the creation of the symbolic record along with the artist, living the experience with him, studying the process wherever it led.[37] He only understands the past who has experienced the same actions as the creators of that period. Thucydides and Machiavelli set this pattern.[38]

Dilthey thus argued that the universal stream of historical continuity was accessible to the human mind. He had shown that the intensive study of the symbolic expression of the stream, such as Hegel and Ranke had undertaken, was the only method of achieving knowledge of the stream. He had argued that the stream arose out of the life-situation in which the mind interacted with the physical and cultural environment. He had shown that the methods of hermeneutics were the means to be used in the study of the process by which the symbolic expressions arose out of the life-situation. Up to this point, Dilthey's system had been approaching a more exact statement of the historical process. Nevertheless, his arguments were still, in a Kantian sense, arguments *a posteriori,* with a presumption, but not a demonstration, of universality and necessity. Dilthey had to give the arguments universality and necessity in order to place the study of the historical process upon a scientific basis. To accomplish this he employed the other stream of thought which came down to him from the Kantian-Fichtean period: the doctrine of the categories of the mind.

---

[36] Misch, "Einleitung," p. xvi.
[37] *Der junge Dilthey,* p. 168.   [38] *Ibid.,* p. 168.

The doctrine of the primacy of the categories of the mind over the universal historical stream furnished Dilthey with a further means of analyzing the historical process. It was a means of giving universality and necessity to the manner in which man's mind worked in history, thus laying the basis for what Dilthey considered to be a sure study of the development of man's culture. According to Dilthey this was the final step in the elevation of the historical human sciences to the level of an exact science.

The consciousness of the primacy of the categories, forms of thought, or schemata over the intellect, was the major heritage from the humanist tradition of German idealism, complementing the concept of the individual as activity. Any attempt at a philosophy of philosophy, at a critique of historical reason, would have to complete Kant's undertaking.[39] The categories had to be looked upon as a driving force in human thought and action, not as limiting goals.[40] They were immanent teleological forces which determined the broad general paths of man's thought and action in history.

If Dilthey could show that the forms of man's thought in the historical stream were an outgrowth of the immanent form which was imprinted upon the continuum by the categories, then he would demonstrate that values and forms of human thought and activity were not only subject to the standards of an age but were also the outgrowth of universal human nature.[41] Dilthey argued that every mind which grasped and comprehended a part of the universal continuum added to the growth of the continuum. The minds which molded the continuum, and thus shaped it in accordance with the forms of the mind, were of the same nature

---

39 *Ibid.,* p. 80.
40 Misch, "Einleitung," p. xxxii.
41 *Der junge Dilthey,* pp. 79-80.

as our minds.   In this way we are enabled to know and to understand other minds as they created history.   The fact that all human minds function in the same formal categories was, for Dilthey, the foundation of a universal science of human thought in history and the demonstration of the possibility of understanding that thought.   "The Kantian investigation of the categories and Fichte's attempt to deduce from them would find a perptuator in the person who could explain the movement of the human mind from the unity of the mental world and explain the primal purposes of that world . . . from the necessities of human nature." [42]   Dilthey felt himself to be that perpetuator.

From a study of the forms of man's actions and thoughts in history, Dilthey tried to explain man's psychological reactions and attitudes to the world.   Out of these psychologically explained forms or types grew world-views. World-views were the result of the giving of content to the forms of the mind by the historical stream.   They were the primary patterns in which the sensory impressions of the external world were organized.   They, therefore, basically determined the thoughts, values and actions of the individual.   In this early stage of the development of his system Dilthey did not make clear the exact manner in which the world-views arose.   He implied that they arose out of the categories.   World-views were the basic ways in which the external world was perceived.   Like Fichte and Goethe, Dilthey argued that one's view of the objective external world was due not to the material of that world itself but to the type of man one was, and one's attitude toward the world.   Goethe wrote:

Every man sees the finished, complete, and organized world only as a starting point out of which he creates a special

[42] *Ibid.*

world which is suitable to his nature. He who is permeated with this basic truth will strive with one truth but will regard the ideas of another, as well as his own, as phenomena.[43]

World-views, then, were not universally valid views of the world, but rather systems of values which were widely shared. Different types of minds would see the world in different ways.

Dilthey believed that there were three basic world views. These were subjective idealism, objective idealism, and naturalism. Each of these was a system of values and a system of knowledge complete in itself, as valid as any other system. A consciousness of the world-view types would lead to scientific certainty.

This method of investigating human thought in history had been demonstrated by Friedrich Schlegel in his analysis of the prose of Lessing and Plato. Schleiermacher endeavored to understand Plato by studying him in relation to a primal world-view.[44] Dilthey wished to formulate even more exactly the types of human outlook upon the world. By 1861 he had distinguished the type of ethical realism of Goethe, Schleiermacher and Lotze, from the idealistic thought of Kant, Fichte, and Herbart. As a result of his study of positivism he added naturalism as a third world-view.[45] Dilthey believed that all human thought fell into one of these three main types of thinking. This was due not to the nature of the external world, but to the categories of the mind.

Dilthey's interpretation of these three world-views grew out of Trendelenburg's typology, which had defined three

---

[43] Heinrich Schmidt, *Philosophisches Wörterbuch* (Leipzig, 1931), p. 429.

[44] Misch, "Einleitung," p. xxxii.

[45] Bernard Groethuysen, "Einleitung," in Dilthey, *Gesammelte Schriften*, VII, 211.

possible attitudes toward the world.[46] (1) The mind could completely impress its forms upon our understanding of nature. Such a view was an idealism of freedom. (2) The mind could act as a mere mirror and completely reflect the natural world, serving only in a passive capacity. This view was a positivistic naturalism. (3) The mind could interact with the environment, partially reflecting the natural world and partially molding it to the understanding. This was the view of the pantheistic life-philosophers which Dilthey admired. He called this world-view an ethical realism, or, later, an objective idealism.

Dilthey then applied the concept of the world-views to the history of ideas. "The history of ideas contains necessary forms," said Dilthey, "not from the nature of the substance, but out of the essence of man." [47] Since world views arose out of the categories of the mind, "the history of ideas has the task of finding the point at which those dark driving forces of the human reason come to light and to follow their influence in all forms." [48] When he was delving into another mind in this fashion he could be sure he was dealing with ascertainable knowledge, not merely with his idea of it, because the universal nature of the mind enabled all minds to understand all other minds. Secondly, he had to recreate the universal-historical continuum of the past age. That continuum was built up out of the individual creative acts of minds, which worked in the same manner as his did. He could, therefore, grasp the reality of the historical stream. Thirdly, it was his duty to find the ways in which the categories of human minds interacted with the historical stream and manifested themselves in concrete historical expressions. In this fashion,

---

[46] Wach, *Die Typenlehre Trendelenburgs,* p. 18.
[47] *Der junge Dilthey,* p. 90.   [48] *Ibid.,* p. 80.

Dilthey evolved a method which would be universal in its application to the historical studies. It would be the basis of a scientific study of the historical sciences in the same sense that Kant's *Critique of Pure Reason* was the basis of the natural sciences.

By demonstrating: (1) that the process of history was the process of the development of ideas out of a life-situation and the progression of action from those ideas, (2) that ideas arose in history within certain necessary and universal types of world-views, and (3) that the investigator's mind could understand those ideas because his mind functioned in similar patterns, Dilthey felt he had achieved a scientifically valid basis for the understanding of the history of ideas.

The method of study of the history of ideas which Dilthey developed was thus a threefold one. First of all, the student had to enter into a like mind in the past by a process of intuition. He had to recreate in his imagination, by a "reflective creative act," the life situation which gave rise to the specific ideas and expressions of the laws of the human mind. Universal knowledge of past history was, therefore, possible. This was the outline of Dilthey's critique of historical knowledge.

IV

DILTHEY'S FINAL

SPECULATIONS

Like all the young men of his generation (the 1860s), Dilthey favored *Realpolitik* as a solution to the "German question" brought into being by the victory of Prussia over Austria. It was a rebellion of sons against their fathers. Dilthey's father was a loyal subject of Nassau; the son was very nearly a disciple of Treitschke.[1] Emotionally Dilthey was willing to be a democrat, "but intellect teaches us to endure a severe form of monarchy." He denigrated the lesser German princes, saying: "If the best interest of the State requires it, they ought to retire on pensions like any ordinary clerk," for monarchist feelings have a meaning only if they serve the German State, "which is, both in war and in politics, in a state of development and in need of strong centralized direction." Therefore, in 1866, Dilthey wholeheartedly favored Bismarck and war, and he continued to believe that the monarchic unity of the Prussian military state should be preserved. By 1870, he insisted that historical judgment must remain free from political passions. He thought it improper for a historian to side with the House of Orange against the Republicans, as Treitschke had done in an essay on Dutch history. Dilthey asserted that the militarists have always been the necessary counterbalance to the forces of peace, commerce, and sci-

[1] Prussia, in 1866, conquered Nassau. Also, soon afterwards, Treitschke accepted a call to Berlin from Heidelberg, which was also situated in a lesser state.

ence; still, the historian must not unite with the militarists, for they wish to transform states into armed fortresses. "The House of Orange by itself would never have been able to create the mild Arminianism, so important to science and freedom of thought, thanks to which Holland became an essential part of European history." [2]

This conception of the relative attitudes of parties is an expression of Dilthey's fundamental antidogmatic attitude, which made him the theorist of the *Weltanschauungen*. In the time of Zeller and Kuno Fischer, he strove to transform the history of philosophy into the history of the moral and religious life of mankind. Dilthey no longer deduced systems one from the other dialectically but regarded them instead as manifestations of spiritual conditions and needs. As an interpreter of human events from a religious and ethical viewpoint, he tended to ignore economic and political problems. He was an historian of metaphysics, which he saw developing or, rather, perpetuating itself through lines of thinkers. History was intuited as a vast life stream, out of which arose immanent forms, and these were expressed in a teleological fashion in the objective creation of the active human mind. Ideas were the expression of the universal mind of man in contact with life. He refused to see a separation between mind and reality. Because reality is the teleological idea, or purpose, and partakes of both mind and being, the mind can come to know the world of reality. Man develops his nature only in the state and in history. The character of man and its growing realization in time was the starting point of world history. For Dilthey, the religious-metaphysical consciousness was the intimate substance of history; to estrange oneself from it was to renounce life.

[2] *Der junge Dilthey*, p. 290.

It is difficult to understand why Dilthey has been likened to Nietzsche.[3] For none of the intolerance, sarcasm, and rebellion of Zarathustra found even an echo in this representative of Protestant spirituality, who lived in the universal church of minds and wrote its history and who, on the eve of his death (May, 1911) said: "From it (the *Aufklärung*)[4] is derived the superiority of our individual outlook on life over that of the greatest thinkers and heroes, of the loftiest religious spirits of the ancient world. For it was on that day that the human race had come to stand on a solid base, facing an actual goal and a sure path thereto."[5]

At the age of twenty-four, Dilthey took upon himself the task of defining the differences between the Graeco-Roman world and the Christian theological systems. Dilthey was primarily concerned with the origin and structure of the European mind. His goal was to understand the historical process, to discover how world-views arose from the giving of content to the structure of the mind by the historical process.[6] An encounter with Schleiermacher's writings provided Dilthey with the first opportunity for the understanding of a world-view. He regarded his study of Schleiermacher as an occasion to examine closely a modern philosopher who was related to those he was then studying— Philo, Scotus Erigena, Lanfranc. He wrote an essay on the

[3] G. Masur, "Wilhelm Dilthey und die europäische Geistesgeschichte," *Deutsche Vierteljahrschrift für Literaturwissenschaft und Geistesgesichte* (1934), Heft 4, p. 502.

[4] Dilthey sharply distinguished the German aspect of the Enlightenment from that of the French and English, and here I use *Aufklärung* to express only the German aspect.

[5] "Das achtzehnte Jahrhundert und die geschichtliche Welt," *Deutsche Rundschau*, May, 1911, reprinted in *Gesammelte Schriften*, III, 224.

[6] *Der junge Dilthey*, pp. 147-48.

hermeneutics of Schleiermacher, tracing a history of al-
legoric interpretation from Crates of Mallos onward. He
realized that the totality of life was the starting point for an
understanding of the basic concepts of hermeneutics. He
imagined an irrational depth of the mind from which
"forms" of thought would emanate. Man was engaged in
a continual process of taking from the stream of history, refining the content in terms of his own interests, and giving
to history the refined product. Psychology and history
would work together in seeking the genesis of systems; history would indicate the points where the primordial impulses have come to the surface, and psychology would
analyze and describe the laws of these natural products,
these "crystallizations" which are the systems.

Dilthey sought to blend romantic transcendental philosophy with the realistic and empirical philosophy of his
time.[7] To be sure, his problem (viz., forcing rebellious
historiography into the context of science after recognizing
its independence from the physical sciences) was a problem of his time. In his work "Ideen über eine beschreibende und zergliedernde Psychologie" (1894),[8] he professed to have realized his goal of reconciling psychology
and science, by vesting historiography with the character
and dignity of science.

Dilthey's concern with history, his belief that it was more
fundamental than philosophy in understanding life itself,
compelled him to seek meaning in history. History was
meaningful, because the minds which molded the continuum, and thus shaped it in accordance with the forms of
mind, were of the same nature as our mind. The ultimate
category of the mind was meaning. History, thus, was the

---

[7] G. Masur, "Wilhelm Dilthey," p. 483.
[8] *Gesammelte Schriften*, Vol. V (Berlin, 1924).

investigation of how the individual mind objectified itself according to the universal and necessary laws of the human mind.

As early as 1859, Dilthey delved into the problem of typology. He proposed to determine the *Grundformen* of ancient thought and the impulses which had made of Christianity a new *Grundform*. But Dilthey wanted to investigate these forms in a scientific manner. The problem for Dilthey was to acquaint himself fully with the findings of science. Dilthey proceeded to study Helmholtz's optics and Fechner's psychophysics. As a professor at Basel, he became interested in psychological research, and he collaborated with a colleague in physiology. This type of study was representative of the great positivistic movement sweeping Germany at the time in which Dilthey was carried along. Comte, another antimetaphysician, was just the person to captivate the mind of the declared enemy of all dogmatism. Positivism satisfied the desire for the concrete, which animated the entire generation. Yet Dilthey felt that he was carrying on some of the ideas originally set forth by Kant. Had not Kant discovered the *Denkformen,* the categories of the mind? And had not Schiller, in his first steps, deduced aesthetic theories from certain universal *Denkformen*? The romanticists had spoken of "style" in more or less analogous terms. Now it was proper to extend the quest, to explain the genesis of these "forms" by means of psychological terms. He agreed with Goethe's assertion that only he who contemplates all forms of existence is a complete man. And, finally, there was also something of Ranke's spirit in Dilthey's desire to systematize all systems, to justify all ideals.

Like scintillating geometric crystals, like musical ideas for a great polyphony, the *Grundformen* did not then have for Dilthey any intrinsic logical necessity, nor any correspondence with eternal reality. How could one escape scepticism? Psychology offered a solid ground. Instead of a single logic, Dilthey strove to produce a classification of forms which evolved and changed, not arbitrarily, but in obedience to the structure of the psyche. Systems of ideas grew up, became self-realized, and took on a life of their own. This self-realization of systems was the ultimate aim of the study of the history of ideas.

Dilthey was not alone in venturing in this direction; Steinthal was writing the "Charakteristik der Grundtypen des menschlichen Sprachbaues," and Lazarus was pursuing his schematic "Völkerpsychologie." Had he been less devoid of scruples, Dilthey would have improvised a "Psychologie der Weltanschauung"; he did not attempt this because the psychological foundation which had seemed so firm at first now vanished under him. The authentic psychological reality which now faced Dilthey was the inner life of the individual, the individual in his unity and totality, which had revealed itself to him while he was reconstructing Schleiermacher's *Nachlass*.

In the Basel *Introduction* (1867) Dilthey declared that poets had taught him to understand the world. The systems of Schelling, Hegel, and Schleiermacher were but logical and metaphysical translations of a *Lebens- und Weltansicht* of a Lessing, a Schiller, and a Herder. The poet is the interpreter of a state of mind, which permeates a generation and crystallizes it into a system. A system lives or dies, not according to reasons of logic, but by virtue of the duration of that state of mind which had originated it.

Dilthey's study of Schleiermacher's personality [9] through his letters, diary, notes, and fragmentary writings, had taught him that to understand means to recreate (*nacherleben*). Schleiermacher himself had said that the *Gemüt*

[9] *Das Leben Schleiermachers,* Vol. I, 1867 (Berlin, 1922).

was the means by which the mind approached the Absolute, and that to comprehend other minds was to identify oneself with them (*sich hineinleben*). These efforts, which were the basis of all forms of metaphysics, were the outgrowth of Schleiermacher's dynamic and emotional life, a life which embodied the spirit of the last great reformation of Protestant religiosity.

Although Dilthey never became a follower of Schleiermacher, his family background and pietistic musical temperament linked him to Schleiermacher and permitted him to enter the latter's world. With a light step, as though afraid of dispelling the enchantment, Dilthey entered Schleiermacher's inner world and succeeded in clarifying the theologian's feelings and affections, so often obscure and complicated. Dilthey felt that in Schleiermacher's thoughts and concepts, there was a lived experience, the *Erlebnis,* an elementary immediate reality.

It has been said: "Dilthey never made it clear to himself whether the *Erlebnis* was a real, artistic intuition or a direct, psychological experience in the sense afforded by descriptive psychology." [10]   Undoubtedly, the concept of *Erlebnis* was ambiguous, for it was at this point that Dilthey tried to relate historical interpretation to psychological description. Dilthey postulated in the structure of the *Erlebnis* the roots of this attitude which later developed into the notions of cognition, affection, and conation. One can almost say that the *Erlebnis* is the closed bud containing all the parts which constitute the flower.[11]   From a study of the forms of man's actions Dilthey tried to explain

[10] G. De Ruggiero, "Note sulla piú recente filosofia europea," *La Critica,* VI (1930), 443.

[11] The word *Erlebnis,* which was in vogue in Germany (as only in Germany words can be in vogue), has no exact English equivalent. Experience is the closest that one can come to it. It can be defined as an event of spiritual vividness.

man's psychological reactions and attitudes to the world. He recognized that some philosophers considered thought a product of the will and acknowledged none but the efficient cause. There were others who interpreted the world in terms of the idea of the whole and saw in efficient cause only the vehicle of formal ends; there were still others who sacrificed neither thought to will nor will to thought. Dilthey gave structure to intellectual history, while he demanded that the structure arise from life and not be imposed. But could the forms of thought comprising the structure satisfy the multiplicity of intellectual expression? If intellectual history is the history of intellectual creativeness, the historian has to acknowledge that he can accomplish more than historical description; he can re-experience and intuit all philosophic thought as the individual mind is merely a different aspect of the same intellectual continuum.

The *Life of Schleiermacher* remains a fragment, although a very remarkable and noteworthy one. Dilthey indicated in the draft of the preface to the second edition, his new contribution: Schleiermacher's relation to Spinoza and to the romanticists. Dilthey discovered that Schleiermacher had been decisively influenced by his intercourse with the romanticists. His position with regard to Schleiermacher's Spinozism was still bolder. Dilthey wrote: "Schleiermacher's religious activity consisted in finding a respectable place for pantheistic mysticism in the bosom of the Church." Thus, the covert accusation of Schleiermacher's adversaries was taken up by the student and transformed into a glorious title of merit. To understand Schleiermacher it was necessary to reconstruct the whole historical period in which he lived; to be at home in the atmosphere in which he worked.

In the person of Schleiermacher Dilthey found the his-

torical problem which concerned him, to wit, the transition
from classical metaphysics to Christian spiritualism. He
believed that these two moments were not so much two historical periods as two *Grundformen* perpetuated throughout history; Christianity is theistic and posits a personal relation between God and man, whereas the world-view of
Schleiermacher's romantic period was a pantheistic monism
which he had absorbed through the medium of Shaftesbury
before becoming acquainted with Spinoza and Bruno.

Thus, the entire history of the modern mind was seen
from new perspectives. Dilthey's approach became completely permeated by the desire to see patterns of thought
dominating the universal history of the mind. The Renaissance was not a period which was absorbed by the Reformation (not even in Germany); it extended throughout the
seventeenth and eighteenth centuries, and was still patent
in romanticism with its pantheistic motives. Protestantism,
with its dogmas of sin, grace, and salvation, was a reas-
sessment of Christian spiritualism; and the ferment of the
modern religious consciousness must be sought in that pantheism which had reappeared in pietism and then tri-
umphed with Schleiermacher.

Dilthey strove to understand Lutheran theology by examining it in its own historical period. Because he realized that the mortifying enslavement of the *Landeskirchen*
was responsible for the decadence of the Lutheran religion,
he came to regard heretics like Spener, Arnold, Francke,
Zinzendorf as "men who had extremely beneficial influence
on the mind and culture of the German nation." This
heterodox religiousness had culminated in Schleiermacher,
a pupil of the *Herrnhuter,* who made a sharp distinction between the free Church, which was the expression of the
universal religious feeling, and the state Church, which was
an expression of the social order.

As a result of studying Schleiermacher's early life in the Brothers' Community, Dilthey began to delve into the history of the German Protestant sects. He discovered the causal relationship between Protestant asceticism and the spirit of economic enterprise in the sixteenth and seventeenth centuries, thus anticipating the famous theories of Max Weber, Troeltsch, and Tawney. For Dilthey this biography signified primarily a splendid example of the construction of a new system, of a new *Weltanschauung,* on the basis of a new, powerful *Erlebnis.* Dilthey believed that biography was the most instructive form for the understanding of life. Through biography one could intuit the origin of ideas and ideals; the history of biography showed both ideas and ideals to be in a continually evolving world of the mind.

Schleiermacher's *Erlebnis* was a characteristic outcome of heterodoxy. He was born in an environment where the yearning for grace filled one's existence. Schleiermacher had found in the Moravian Community not only the yearning but the certainty, the sentimental and visionary enjoyment of grace. The Lutheran conception of certainty, an inner process manifesting the guarantee of salvation, had there become a spiritual mood—a *Gemüt.* Jesus was felt and enjoyed as the constantly present spouse of the exalted soul. The form of worship was an anticipation on earth of the celestial beatitudes—liturgical chants and the splendor of candles, ecstatic raptures and tender tears. In noting the analogy between this type of religious feeling and the Catholic mysticism of Love, Dilthey was one of the first to describe that form of mentality which is called baroque. Thus, in Schleiermacher the *Erlebnis* appeared essentially as the gentle *Gemüt,* the irrational nucleus from which poetry, music, religion, and philosophy sprang. *Erlebnis* was for Dilthey the universal premise for every biographical, critical, and historical interpretation. The historian must be able to feel and then intuit the source of creativeness of the individual he studies. Dilthey thought that the irrational, individual life could be relived only by virtue of an intimate communion of the self with the mind of the individual studied. Acknowledging the limitations of the mind's expressive forms, the historian must then try to understand the forms into which these various expressions fall. In the case of Schleiermacher, the new world-view was determined by the *Aufklärung* and Kant, by Spinoza and the romanticists. Subjective idealism was thus the dominating form.

This meeting of mysticism and pantheism was made possible by the *Aufklärung*. Dilthey reinterpreted the *Aufklärung* to include the history of the Protestant religion. The Enlightenment was empirical and utilitarian, and severed all ties between God and men. The *Aufklärung,* on the contrary, although it abandoned the old dogmas, exalted the order of the universe, the progressive education of the human race, the moral betterment of individuals, and it preserved, nay, purified, the Christian intuitive notion of the relation between Creator and creatures. Many thinkers have tried to understand the Christian character, but few have, as Dilthey has, dared to proclaim the heirs of the Christian religion those very individuals whom orthodoxy regards as its most dangerous foes.

In an essay on Lessing [12] Dilthey defined the new *Erlebnis* of the *Aufklärung*. This *Erlebnis* envisioned a free society which, despite the diversity of races and religions, would realize happiness. The Lutheran anguish of sin would vanish, and the new science would renew man's confidence in his powers. From this *Weltansicht* of liberation were born Schiller's *Don Carlos*, Kant's philosophy of reli-

[12] *Das Erlebnis und die Dichtung* (Leipzig, 1921).

gion, Herder's concept of humanity, and Beethoven's Ninth Symphony. Lessing was the perennial symbol of the modern German mind.

The *Life of Schleiermacher,* together with essays on Hölderlin and Novalis, reprinted in *Das Erlebnis und die Dichtung,* formed a substantial reevaluation of the first romantic generation. Compared with Rudolf Haym's [13] massive study of the romantic movement, Dilthey's work was more sympathetic. He spoke not of a school, but of a "generation," varied as individuals can vary, but united by a common moral purpose, by common exigencies and problems. To Dilthey, the romanticists appeared primarily as the promoters of revolutionary moral concepts, subverters of the traditional ethical dogmas.

Dilthey rejected Hegel's dialectical evolution but accepted his belief in the unity of European civilization. For Hegel, history was the process of the spirit becoming conscious of its own self, of its cumulative concept of itself. Hegel saw history teleologically and excluded all the contingent, tracing the grand outline only of the cosmic drama whose human detail was often tragedy. Dilthey denied any such philosophical interpretation of history and saw the ideal essence of the history of the human race in the task which "the history of ideas has of finding the point at which those dark driving forces of the human reason come to light and of following their influence in all forms." [14] The revelation of the poet, prophet, and creator of a new *Erlebnis* provided the subject matter of historiography. Dilthey denied "progress" in the sense of a universal guiding reason promoting the development of the human race from one stage to the next, or of a spiritual character inherent in

---

13 Rudolf Haym, *Die romantische Schule* (Berlin, 1870).
14 *Der junge Dilthey,* p. 80.

man that would, of necessity, drive matters toward a final goal. Since reality was infinite, many-sided, and the types of world-views were necessarily limited, progress toward a better apprehension of the aspects of reality, toward a more unbiased outlook upon existence, toward a more humane humanity, was possible only in the domain of the *Erlebnisse,* of which the poets were the interpreters. The *Aufklärung* of a Lessing and the romanticism of a Schlegel and a Schleiermacher were not for Dilthey antithetic terms but two successive *Erlebnisse* which complemented each other. Dilthey was able to show how each new *Erlebnis* manifested itself in a new generation and then underwent various transformations. The substance of history, which is composed of *Erlebnisse,* is infinitely diversified and mutable. It is this substance which gives life to Dilthey's historiography, and not the essential forms he professed to be dealing with.

In 1883, Dilthey abandoned writing Schleiermacher's biography and prepared to defend the autonomy of the human studies (Geisteswissenschaften). For the rest of his life Dilthey was concerned with the problem of the scientific value of historiography. In this field he remained as hostile to dogmatism as he had always been. In his view, the historical and social sciences had been throughout the eighteenth century the servants of metaphysics; they had been emancipated by the historical school, but they lacked philosophical justification; now, with the advent of positivism the social sciences were once again in danger of becoming tools of metaphysics. If there was to be any science of history, it was only possible because history had its own peculiar and specific subject matter. It must be demonstrated that a certain realm of appearance exists, for the understanding of which none of the other approaches to knowledge was suited—neither the theological, the philosophical, the mathematical, or physical approach.   Here questions arise which theological or philosophical speculation cannot answer.   These are questions that cannot be logically derived from general principles, but which must be understood and for whose understanding the development of their own intellectual method is required.   In the attempt to preserve the validity of the social sciences, Dilthey wrote in 1883, the *Einleitung in die Geisteswissenschaften.*

Since the time of Lotze's *Mikrokosmus* (1869), the excesses of naturalism had been decried.   Dilthey's originality consisted in using the very criteria of positivism as weapons against the intrusion of naturalism into historical studies.   Less a positivist than positivistic, he refused to submit the substance of inner experience to irrelevant laws and methods.   Like Bergson, another disciple of positivism, he appealed to the immediate data of consciousness.   But, once he had ascertained the particular nature of inner experience, Dilthey did not stray very far from positivism. He set out to find the psychic laws which govern the "moral sciences" (a term he borrowed from John Stuart Mill).

Dilthey intended to accomplish in the "moral sciences" what Kant had done for the mathematical and physical sciences.   The title, *Critique of Historical Judgment,* which he wanted to give his work, contributed to the illusion that this was what he did.   Actually his ideas are inimical to Kantian idealism.   The science he envisioned was a type of descriptive psychology, derived from empirical data which ultimately would become the laws of "psychic structure." In this structure psychology was the basis of every "moral science."   It must determine the general and uniform properties of individuals, while remaining within the realm of description, avoiding hypotheses.   Such a task had hitherto been obstructed by nebulous entities: science, state, society, religion, nation, national soul, national consciousness. For Dilthey, only individuals and their relations with one another were real.

It proved necessary, therefore, to create a new psychology. Dilthey found fault with associationist psychology because it perceived in spiritual life only representations, while real representation was an event, permeated by feelings and interests.[15] The stimuli of the external world provoked representations; feelings intervened and awakened the impulses of the will. The partition of psychic elements into three main types (cognition, emotion, and conation) was for Dilthey a matter of inner experience so irrefutable that he never attempted to justify it critically. He conceded that, within the psychic mechanism, one class is derived from the other. The psychologist, however, must avoid formulating hypotheses, and refrain from attempting to penetrate the sanctum of psychic experience.

At first Dilthey believed that he could build on these premises the foundation of aesthetics, which he considered one of the "moral sciences." Since feeling distinguished poetry, the analysis of feelings would create aesthetic laws. Fechner had deduced laws from the effects wrought on the spectator by a work of art. Dilthey endeavored to extract the same "supreme principles" from the description and classification of emotional reactions. He soon realized, however, that art was not only emotion, but vision, and that trying to reduce it to rules was invalid. "There comes a genius who makes everyone see as he sees, and creates a school, a style, an epoch."[16] By inviting us to share a new

[15] Dilthey, *Die Einbildungskraft des Dichters* (1887), in *Gesammelte Schriften*, Vol. VI.

[16] Dilthey, *Die drei Epochen der modernen Aesthetik und ihre heutige Aufgabe* (1892), in *Gesammelte Schriften*, Vol. VI.

experience, the artist afforded us "a sense of liberty and serenity." For Dilthey, the vitality and the creativity of the soul, which was the root of art, became the only positive reality.

But could Dilthey lose himself in this stream of the irrational? Having overcome the conceptual obstacles, he found before him the pure experience, the *Erlebnis,* just as another radical empiricist, Mach, had found pure sensation. In a descriptive and analytic psychology Dilthey sought a firm basis, comparable to the Cartesian *Cogito,* from which he could analyze rules and procedures. To fall a prey to capricious and subjective psychology would result in the crumbling of all the "moral sciences," which are permeated with psychological notions and operate by virtue of the concepts of will, liberty and imagination.[17]

Another reason for Dilthey's study of psychological procedure was his need to lay the ghost of relativism in historicism. Dilthey wrote: "The wisdom of an era is always a transitory, subjective expression of a state of mind; metaphysical systems and ethical and religious ideals are historically conditioned products, and they vary with time."[18] Dilthey refused to surrender himself to relativism. An objective reality, independent of states of mind, was necessary in order to live and to act. However, since it was not possible to transcend historical actuality, we must seek salvation in our historical consciousness. In the multiplicity of conceptions of the world, we must seek the uniform structure of existence. It became necessary to trace these structures of existence back to the life of the *Ego* from which they emanated. Thus, history was inseparable from psychology;

---

[17] Dilthey, *Erfahren und Denken* (1892), in *Gesammelte Schriften,* Vol. V.

[18] Dilthey, *Das geschichtliche Bewusstsein und die Weltanschauungen,* in *Gesammelte Schriften,* Vol. III.

and hence the relativity and subjectivity of philosophical systems was reaffirmed; while, on the other hand, historicism was rejected.

Before searching for the uniform structures in the history of systems, Dilthey tried to understand the living consciousness in order to observe its conduct.[19] Could the intellect approach the immediate reality of life? Dilthey admitted that whatever we experienced within ourselves could not be clear to the intellect, nay, that vital processes appeared as contradictory when submitted to the intellect for judgment. Dilthey did not indulge in mystical visions. Forced to choose between *Erlebnis* and science, he chose the latter. He no longer regarded the *Erlebnis* as an unrehearsed and nondescript event, as a mere inner vibration, but charged it with all the weight of the intellect. If in the rapid course of inner processes we isolate one such process, he argued, we would perceive in it inter-relations and constant functions. These very habits of the psyche were explained as logical, elementary operations. The intellect was born of the *Erlebnis*; the abstract was living and present in the concrete. When the intellect, according to its nature performed its task of differentiation, it defined a reality which was already a structure, a life which was already a mass of functions. Psychological abstraction had a sure guide in this spontaneous self offering of an interior order, and if it reached certain hypotheses, these had the *Erlebnis* as their starting point.[20]

[19] Dilthey, *Ideen über eine beschreibende und zergliedernde Psychologie* (1894), in *Gesammelte Schriften*, Vol. V.

[20] Recently many attempts have been made to interpret Dilthey's philosophy and to organize it into a metaphysical system: see G. Misch, *Lebensphilosophie und Phänomenologie*, 2d ed. (Leipzig and Berlin, 1931); O. F. Bollnow, "Die Lehre von den Typen der Weltanschauung," in *Neue Jahrbücher für Wissenschaft und Jugendbildung*, 1934, Heft 4; J. Stenzel, "Dilthey und die deutsche Philosophie der Gegenwart," in

In 1894 Windelband discovered ambiguities in Dilthey's thinking. In the course of a lecture on history and natural science, Windelband observed that psychology was intrinsically a naturalistic science because it was concerned with laws, whereas historiography dealt with the particular. Dilthey explained that the peculiar end of the natural sciences was not the search for law but for causality; if the sciences which formulated laws were naturalistic, then not only historiography, but also politics, economics, linguistics, aesthetics, and generally speaking all the "moral sciences," should be termed natural sciences. Instead, Dilthey main-

---

Philosophische Vorträge der Kant-Gesellschaft, Vol. XXXIII (Berlin, 1934); D. Bischoff, *W. Diltheys geschichtliche Lebensphilosophie* (Leipzig and Berlin, 1934). These writers have asserted that, since Dilthey uses the words *Weltanschauung* and *Lebensanschauung* interchangeably, he must believe that "Ego" and "world" are indissolubly united in life. This is not so because Dilthey did not use *Weltanschauung* and *Lebensanschauung* interchangeably. He used *Weltanschauung* to indicate a prevalence of the cognitive, and *Lebensanschauung* to emphasize the affective moment. Since neither moment ever exists completely without the other, Dilthey can freely use both words, while having recourse at times, for the sake of accuracy, to the expression *Welt- und Lebensansicht.*

When Dilthey says that pure inner life and the pure external world are never given, but always present themselves as bound in a vital nexus, he merely enunciates the obvious principle that there is no subject without object, and vice-versa. However, he gives to this principle a psychological meaning. He never denies Fecher's psychology, which he had studied as a youth: external stimuli act on the consciousness, which in turn reacts with feelings and volitional acts. There exists, then, for Dilthey, a continuous relation of action-reaction, between the "Ego" and the environment, in a physiopsychological sense. At times he expresses hope that life may afford us some indication of an objective reality, but he never goes any farther. At any rate, the two terms, "Ego" and "world" always remain for him two distinct entities, even though life is substantially a communion of the two: objective reality escapes our direct approach, and life does not embrace nor understand it. To persist in asserting that, in Dilthey's vocabulary, "life" and "world" are practically interchangeable is equivalent to ascribing to some sporadic phrases (contained in his manuscript notes) a weight and a meaning which Dilthey's general philosophy goes to contradict.

tained that the peculiarity of these sciences consisted in the relation between the particular and objective realities expressed in laws.[21]

Dilthey thus faced the problem of what constitutes knowledge of the individual. How was it possible to know the individual scientifically? As a young man, Dilthey had studied the history of hermeneutics, and now he saw in this science the means to understand the "moral sciences" better. Any form of historical-philological knowledge is based on the assumption that understanding attains objectivity. It therefore was necessary to determine the rules of such a process in order to ascertain the authenticity of the interpretation.[22]

For Dilthey, dealing with hermeneutics meant a return to Schleiermacher. To be sure, Schleiermacher had taught him that understanding was penetrating into someone's spiritual life, a *Sich-hineinversetzen,* an act which was followed by a *Nachbilden* or a *Nacherleben,* a reproduction or re-living. Could one confine oneself to this simple re-living? The "moral sciences," said Dilthey, did not merely offer a copy of a given reality, but they actually reconstructed it by means of abstract conceptual relations.[23] Thus Dilthey returned to the point from which he had departed. In order to validate the understanding scientifically, he was led to postulate a theory of the psychic structure. He sought in psychic life the regular and uniform relations, and he placed hermeneutics in the domain of descriptive psychology.

Only toward the end of his life did Dilthey seem to make

---

[21] Dilthey, *Beiträge zum Studium der Individualität* (1896), in *Gesammelte Schriften,* V, 264-65.

[22] Dilthey, *Die Enstehung der Hermeneutik* (1900), in *Gesammelte Schriften,* Vol. V.

[23] Dilthey, *Zur seelischen Struktur* (1905), in *Gesammelte Schriften,* Vol. V.

an effort to extend the scope of his work. He no longer spoke of functions, relations, structures, but of categories; he emphasized the category of meaning, or significance, in the process of understanding. He maintained that this category was synonymous with life and that the problem was to render the category of meaning intelligible by giving it order and form.[24] It is not, therefore, a Kantian category peculiar to the understanding mind, but an objective relation of the psychic structure.

This new category was often hailed as a novelty, as if Dilthey had only just discovered that to re-live is not sufficient to construct history. But, as we have seen, the problem of extracting from the *Erlebnis* the forms of conceptual knowledge had always preoccupied him. The new element in his thought was his exclusive concern with the problem of historiography. Even his investigation of the construction of the historical world was only a renewal of his old attempt to establish the "moral sciences" and the objective value of their contribution.[25]

Dilthey's procedure was still that of descriptive and analytical psychology; to understand was to inwardly assimilate; consequently, the categories of understanding must correspond to the categories of life, the life which was being apprehended; they must be traced in the individual *Erlebnis* and be extended to all individuals, so that they might establish their worth as categories of the spiritual world.[26] Thus, the task of the historian was not mastered by intellect alone; it required, rather, a constant coöperation of the creative imagination, which alone could unify

[24] Dilthey, *Die Abgrenzung der Geisteswissenschaften,* in *Gesammelte Schriften,* Vol. V.

[25] Dilthey, *Der Aufbau der geschichtlichen Welt* (1910), in *Gesammelte Schriften,* Vol. V.

[26] Dilthey, *Entwürfe zur Kritik der historischen Vernunft,* in *Gesammelte Schriften,* Vol. VII.

isolated and widely dispersed facts. The historian's imagination does not strive to transcend reality. It subordinates itself to experience and to the investigation of what
is real. History, therefore, is not merely a special province
but the whole of reality. All history is contemporary history; thus history and philosophy become one. There is
no realm of being, no other subject matter for philosophical thought beyond the human realm of history.

In the essay, "On the Importance of Archives in the
Study of Philosophy " (1899), Dilthey examined the relation between the history of civilization and the history of
philosophy. The philosophical systems, he said, represent
the civilization of a people and of an era inasmuch as they
raise life to the plane of conscious thought and subsequently influence the conduct of individuals and societies.
The history of philosophy clarifies the phases of man's spiritual life, and fixes the products of literature, theology, and
science in history.

At first glance, it would seem that Dilthey assigned to
thought a central historical function. But this was not so.
What then was it that determined the movement of
thought? Not an intrinsic contradiction, not an immanent
principle, but the successive modifications of the "sense of
life" (*Lebensgefühl*) caused the movement of thought.
From each change of the *Lebensgefühl* the philosopher,
like the artist and the religious reformer, drew his reason
for being. Philosophy was the symbolic projection of a
state of mind; it had no life of its own.

For Dilthey the dualism of *Lebensgefühl* and metaphysics represents the progressive liberation of mankind, or at
least of European society. Already the first volume of the
Einleitung in die Geisteswissenschaften contained a historical section which illustrated the decadence of metaphysics.

Before proceeding to found a truly modern scientific philosophy free of rationalistic substructures, he wanted to demonstrate that the entire development of modern thought was reducing man to psychological description. The second volume of the *Einleitung* was to deal with the discovery of the individual during the Renaissance and the Reformation and, consequently, with the natural system of the moral sciences which took shape in the seventeenth century.[27] Actually, Dilthey was able to write only a few of the preparatory essays.[28]

The Renaissance, according to Dilthey, illustrated the spectacular dissolution of medieval metaphysics, followed by an affirmation of a new *Lebensgefühl*. Feudalism and the Church declined; the middle-classes and national states arose; the whole of Europe was engaged in commerce and industry which were being constantly stimulated by new inventions and discoveries. Great men arose to express their genius in great literatures of characters, of feelings, of passions. Dilthey's view of the Renaissance was Shakespearian. We do not encounter a single simple "type" such as Burckhardt's "Renaissance Man," but a stupendous flowering of great personalities of diverse types.

The residue of Protestant animosity against the Renaissance, which one feels even in a Burckhardt, was negligible in Dilthey, who regarded the hedonism of that era as a secondary aspect of the vigorous affirmation of man's autonomy. For him the greatest conquest of the Renaissance was the secularization of the moralistic medieval literature, which began with Petrarch and reached a climax with Machiavelli and Montaigne. Only after the Renaissance

[27] G. Misch in his Introduction to Vol. II of Dilthey, *Gesammelte Schriften* (Leipzig and Berlin, 1921), p. vi.

[28] Dilthey, *Weltanschauung und Analyse des Menschen seit Renaissance und Reformation,* in *Gesammelte Schriften,* Vol. II.

had freed science from the fetters of dogma was it possible to arrive, in the seventeenth century, at man's superiority over nature, and at the conception of a natural system of laws, of politics, of morals, of theology.

What did the Reformation signify in this progressive liberation of minds? Certainly Luther appeared to him to have broken through medieval dogmatism; to be the cause of a turbulent theological upheaval. Dilthey conceded that Luther created a new kind of certitude leading to the emancipation of the mystic experience, of the religious *Erlebnis*. Dilthey's originality consisted in his refutation of Protestant historiography's claim that the Reformation was a return to early Christianity.[29] The expectation of Christ's Kingdom, the basis of Paul's faith, did not affect the reformers who opposed the Anabaptists, heralds of that Kingdom. In reviewing historiography of the Reformation, Dilthey transcended every sectarian attitude; he believed it to be impossible to understand Protestantism without Catholicism and its contribution. Dilthey clearly pointed out, before Max Weber and Troeltsch, that Protestantism, far from eliminating the ascetic ideal of Catholicism, gave it new strength and scope.

Dilthey declared that the progressive victory of humanistic rationalism over Lutheranism and Calvinism was the result of the formulation of the seventeenth century doctrine of "natural light." For Dilthey neither Catholicism nor Protestantism, but the universalistic theism of the humanists (represented by Erasmus' serene and tolerant "philosophy of Christ") was the basis of the new secular faith. This system evolved from the *De Libero Arbitrio* of Erasmus through Coornhert, the Socinians and Arminians, till the time of the Deists. This theism suffused the Reformation in Zwingli and Melanchthon; it communed with

---

[29] Dilthey, *Zur Würdigung der Reformation,* in *Gesammelte Schriften,* Vol II.

German mysticism in the person of Sebastian Franck; and this identification of *lumen naturale* with "Christ invisible within us" was the starting point of German philosophy.

Intellectual progress was only apparent for if medieval metaphysics were dead, other equally fatal metaphysics replaced it. The humanistic *Lebensgefühl*, which seemed so detrimental to metaphysics, did not destroy, but merely determined the dispersion of the three elements, which united in medieval metaphysics. These elements were the religious (the relation between the individual soul and the living God, which passed into the Reformation), the logical-mathematical (the Hellenic contemplation of the cosmos, surviving in Grotius, Descartes and Spinoza) and the Roman (the dominating and co-ordinating volition which is embodied in Machiavelli).

Dilthey felt that there had been no intellectual progress during the Renaissance. There had only been a rearrangement of the same motives. The Renaissance was not a liberation from metaphysics, but a freeing of new metaphysical elements from the ties which had kept them united in the Middle Ages. The liberating analysis of man, which Dilthey saluted in Machiavelli, was also linked to a metaphysical motive.

Since the era of systems had by no means ended with the Renaissance and the seventeenth century, and since metaphysics was being revived again, Dilthey could only return to his pristine ideas of the schematic forms of thought, the "crystallography" of metaphysics. The three elements of medieval metaphysics ceased to belong to a definite historical period; they attained universal significance as "types," or eternal fundamental forms.

Dilthey's three "types" are the following: objective idealism, or the aesthetic and contemplative attitude; the idealism of liberty, or the consciousness of responsibility; and

naturalistic realism. Dilthey found them under different
names in the systems of the nineteenth century: in the
idealism of Schelling, in the spiritualism of Maine de Biran,
in the positivism of Comte and Spencer.[30]

Dilthey had given up psychological analysis for a direct
contemplation of history. It was only through history,
through its experiences and creations, that we could attain
a knowledge of the human mind; only this historical self-
consciousness permitted us to formulate a systematic theory
of man. There must be three types of philosophical systems, because there are also "three moments of the mind";
naturalism parallels knowledge, objective idealism corresponds to affective emotions, and the idealism of liberty
corresponds to volition. They are equivalent in value, as
are the three types, each of which is the realization of a
sole possibility, the expression of a single aspect of reality.
Each type is legitimate. Of course, if it transcends its
limits, it falls into contradiction. We can comprehend the
world solely under one category at a time—of being and of
cause, of value, of purpose, but we can never hope to ap-
prehend the entire system.[31]

Why did Dilthey assume that the universe could be apprehended only through the medium of the "types?" Not
only did he not endeavor to demonstrate the connection between the three categories and reality, but, in the last analysis, he denied this connection by proclaiming elsewhere
that the multisidedness of the universe is infinite. Nor
does he face the problem of the raison d'être of the world-
view, the burden from which man is unable to free himself.

[30] Dilthey, *Die drei Grundformen der Systeme in der ersten Hälfte
des 19 Jahrhunderts*, in *Gesammelte Schriften*, Vol. IV.

[31] Dilthey, *Das Wesen der Philosophie* (1907), in *Gesammelte Schriften*, Vol. V; recently translated by S. A. and W. T. Emery, *The Essence
of Philosophy* (Chapel Hill, 1954).

Only in an essay published on the eve of his death [32] did Dilthey define the world-view. It is an image of the world (*Weltbild*) which determines the value of life (*Lebenserfahrung*) and, consequently, establishes a practical ideal (*Lebensideal*). By its own nature, the world-view defines the immediate experiences of life and gives them form. Again it is clear that Dilthey wants to maintain the tripartition of cognition, affection, and conation.

What differentiates the world-views and determines the prevalence of one type over the others is not the predominance of one of the three "moments," but a unilateral accentuation of subjective life, a sort of unbalancing in the very core of life. "Life" (*Lebendigkeit*), prior to the world-view, is in itself an attitude toward the external world, determined by a particular intention, or mood of the soul. In the last analysis, it is this irrational attitude which gives life its color, and which projects and consolidates itself into a system.

Then the question arises: if life already has a direction to follow, if it is so powerful as to create a *Weltbild*, what then is the purpose of the order which the world-view would provide? One cannot say that the world-view is an intellectual product, for Dilthey encloses in it all three moments of spiritual life: cognition, affection, and conation. The partial truth of every world-view appears even less justified, for a world-view should reveal an aspect of reality. However, one fails to see a connection between such an aspect and the capricious mood, the subjective tone of life.

Did Dilthey then destroy the faith in the rationality of the real? In truth, nothing authorizes us to ascribe to him ideas which are imputed to Nietzsche, with whom he

---

[32] *Die Typen der Weltanschauung und ihre Ausbildung in den metaphysischen Systemen* (1911), in *Gesammelte Schriften*, Vol. VIII.

heartily disagreed. Of course, Dilthey declared that the various sides of reality refuse to enter into a unifying picture. The possibility of contemplating all such sides at once is denied us. The light of truth is visible to us only as a refracted ray. But this impossibility is due to an imperfection of our vision, not to reality itself, which Dilthey imagines to be compact and coherent.[33]

Dilthey found the proof of his theory of "types" in the history of philosophy where they constantly clash, with no hope of a solution. He regarded these "types" as driving forces in human thought and action. They were immanent, teleological forces which determined the broad general path of man's thought and action in history. This theory indicates that Dilthey was greatly influenced by Hegel's concept of spirit. But in Dilthey's history of philosophy there was no becoming; the "types" are always the same. The course of thought is represented not by forces in evolution, but by three lines which, from time to time, cross one another and along which the individual thinkers figure as points of a topographical map on a single plane.[34]

[33] Dilthey, "Traum," in *Gesammelte Schriften,* VIII, 218-24 (see complete translation of this essay in the Appendix).

[34] In 1905 Dilthey began to write a biography of Hegel, which he abandoned after the first few chapters. As he had done for the youth of Schleiermacher, he reconstructed Hegel's youth from the *Nachlass.* In 1888, when reviewing the edition of Hegel's letters, he wrote: "The time of strife has passed; it is now the time for approaching Hegel historically; this historical investigation shall separate what is living and what is dead in him." Dilthey's contribution to Hegelian studies is analogous to his contribution to the understanding of Schleiermacher; in Hegel's life he discovered an early period, a period of mystic pantheism, previously unknown.

The polemic motive of this Hegel biography is worth noting. Dilthey's aim was to refute the originator of the dialectical method not *ex ore suo* but *e vita sua*; he demonstrated that Hegel was less a direct descendant of Fichtean thought than a sum of many factors, the foremost of which was classical pantheism, borrowed from Shaftesbury and

Practically, Dilthey acknowledged progress (but below the stereotyped metaphysical levels) in the *Lebensgefühl,* which becomes ever richer, ever more intense, ever more universally humane. Still, his recognition of progress is postulated rather than proved. When Dilthey describes a new *Lebensgefühl,* he is forced to limit it to a "type." What he offers us is not the ineffable "sense of life" but a philosophy, a *Weltanschauung.* The naturalistic concept of "type" not only renders historiography schematic, but reduces it to sociology.

The most noteworthy example of typological historiography is afforded by Dilthey's essays on the German mind. The young Dilthey had rejected as an abstraction the romantic concept of national consciousness. In his last years, however, he devoted his historical research to the study of the formation of the German national genius. In 1900, he published an essay on Leibniz, Frederick II, and the *Aufklärung,* which he planned to incorporate into a larger study of the history of German thought from Leibniz to Schleiermacher.[35] Then he realized that in order to grasp fully the German *Wesen* it would be necessary for him to return to Luther, or even to medieval poetry and to the most ancient traditions.[36]

What Dilthey means by the essence of the German mind is explained by his discoveries. He recognized the importance of seventeenth century Catholic mysticism, which

---

Hemsterhuys, which had also influenced Schleiermacher. Such pantheism in Hegel was definitely more mystical in character, and it allowed Hegel to meditate upon St. John's Gospel (whence his conception of "spirit"—*Geist*), Eckart, and Tauler and to organize a system similar to that of Plotinus.

[35] P. Ritter, in the Introduction to *Studien zur Geschichte des deutschen Geistes,* in Dilthey, *Gesammelte Schriften* (Leipzig and Berlin, 1927), Vol. III.

[36] Dilthey, *Von deutscher Dichtung und Musik* (Leipzig and Berlin, 1933).

entered Germany with the *Kirchenlied* of Spee and Silesius, and joined with the existent pietistic religious consciousness. When the *Kirchenlied* declined, the pietistic experience found expression in Klopstock and in the music of Bach and Handel.[37]

Heir, not renouncer, of this religious spirit, is the *Aufklärung,* which disintegrates the old dogmas in order to purify the imperishable essence of Christianity. It is this religious character of the *Aufklärung* which inspired Frederick's educational State, and "it is this Christian moral conception, beacon of Stein and of the great leaders of the Wars of Liberation, which endowed the German people with their power of resistance." [38]   The historiography of the nineteenth century is a continuation of the *Aufklärung.* Despite their opposition to rationalism, Niebuhr, Grimm, Hegel, and Ranke are the followers of Semler, Lessing, and Spittler.   By and large, the entire eighteenth century, falsely accused of lacking the historical sense, appears to Dilthey as the originator of a great historical idea, that of the solidarity of the human race, and its progress toward ever greater perfection.   "Thanks to the historical works of Voltaire, Hume, and Gibbon, historicism thrived in the nineteenth century." [39]

The essence of the German mind, in short, was for Dilthey "an idealism of liberty."   Introduced by the individualism of the primitive Germanic tribes, it underwent a continuous process of purification as the Christian history of Germany evolved.   It is in this sense that Dilthey must be interpreted.   Just as Schleiermacher considered himself a *Herrnhuter* of a higher order, Dilthey felt that he was a

[37] *Ibid.*

[38] Dilthey, *Friedrich der Grosse und die deutsche Aufklärung,* in *Gesammelte Schriften,* Vol. III.

[39] *Ibid.*   See the development of this idea by F. Meinecke, *Die Enstehung des Historismus* (München, 1936).

Christian, a partaker of a sort of lay religion, liberated from dogmatic fetters by Kant and Schleiermacher. Progress for Dilthey meant a greater freedom for Christianity. He believed that total freedom could be attained only when all Church dogmas, all systems of philosophy, all artistic creations became symbols of a profound reality which we experience directly in life, in which the consciousness of our superior nature is interwoven with our relations with the Invisible. Like Sebastian Franck, a humanist and a mystic, Dilthey considered himself "independent of all sects, a member of an invisible community, like Socrates and Seneca." This deep-rooted tolerance, this sovereignty of the mind over the systems, "the blessedness of the supreme freedom and mobility of the soul," were for him the highest aim of man. The anxious desire of the young Dilthey to cast away formulas found its fulfillment in history. "The historical consciousness breaks the last chains which philosophy and natural science were unable to break. Now man is completely free." [40]

But was such complete freedom possible? In order to direct his own life, Dilthey considered a world-view indispensable and inevitable. Therefore, he advised that one should quietly pursue one's own world-view, provided that one recognized the equal worth of another world-view. Dilthey opined that an uncompromising attachment to one's own dogmas was a prejudice against the manifoldness of life. Dilthey never asked himself whether it was possible to affirm a world-view while conceding its equality with other world-views. It may not be valid to choose among the three types. Indeed, the situation would be tragic if the irrational *Stimmung* did not intervene to suggest a choice, and to make such a choice appear not only plausible, but necessary.

[40] "Traum", in *Gesammelte Schriften,* Vol. VIII.

Dilthey intended to furnish a philosophical justification for the work of the historical school. On this account, he is regarded as the theorist of that moderate spiritualism of nineteenth century German historiography which had its roots in Humboldt. Actually, Dilthey represents, in the second half of the century, the efforts made by German historical scholarship to free itself of positivism. While his contemporaries believed that they possessed objectivity in documentation, he sought the criteria of certitude in the mind. Consequently, when the naive faith in the *Tatsache* subsided, he appeared as a savior to those who refused to yield to the whims of subjectivism.

Spirituality, however, was but one aspect of Dilthey's nature. The philosopher was also loyal to the positive sciences and to the spirit of rationalism. These three elements (spiritualism, positivism, rationalism) clashed with one another. He sought to reconcile them in the undivided ground of the *Erlebnis,* but he failed to solve the conflict. Since all three were truths for him, he concluded that they should be regarded as partial and contradictory aspects of a higher reality, from which we were excluded. His inability to overcome this internal dissension, the weakness of his thought, caused him to propound the theory of types.

There was, however, the glorious tradition of the *Aufklärung* to make his work as a historian an affirmation of the values of the mind. Thus art, religion, and philosophy could only point the way to something else, to man who expresses himself in them. All their utterances were to be regarded as answers to man's question about himself. Yet we cannot reconcile all the answers to this question. Only by reflective understanding can man become conscious of the unity of man. This unity is found in reflective consciousness, a correlate of the original unity of life, which had been given different modes of expression. Thus to the unity of human experience corresponds the unity to be found in a reflective, philosophical understanding, and only in such an understanding can man grasp the totality of human experience. Here Dilthey found a unity which none of the separate modes of expression could give him. Here he overcame the one-sidedness of each particular attitude. He grasped the common meaning of these different attitudes as he sought through them to understand man who expressed himself in them. He found in images, ideas, and meditations ways in which human life achieved expression.

In his last years he devoted his attention to the German national consciousness, and he wrote that the methods of German education should not be borrowed from the English or from a generic psychology, but from the national *ethos*.[41] This he understood and meant in the spirit of Lessing and Herder. His optimism was that of the eighteenth century. To his faith in the *Aufklärung* he remained true; he did not profess himself a Christian in the exact sense, but, nonetheless, he regarded with utter disgust the attempts to reduce Christianity to an isolated, individual historical fact.[42] His true purpose in defending the autonomy of the *Geisteswissenschaften,* he said, was to guarantee the independence of ethical-religious motives.[43] This was the substance of his doctrine of the *Erlebnis*. Although Dilthey's insight had been gained through poetry, it was the religious experience, the "spark" of the mystics, which he had in mind when he wrote: "The heroic and religious side of human nature transcends metaphysics." [44]

This reverential awe for the mystery of life, this sense of

[41] Dilthey, *Pädagogik, Geschichte und Grundlinien des Systems,* in *Gesammelte Schriften,* Vol. IX.

[42] *Briefwechsel zwischen W. Dilthey und dem Grafen P. York von Wartenburg* (Halle, 1923), p. 125.

[43] *Ibid.,* p. 139.   [44] *Ibid.,* p. 146.

the sacred in human experience, and the consequent history of this experience, mark Dilthey's criticism and historical writings as works of genius. While around him philological erudition was losing itself in superficial detail, he revitalized literary criticism by interpreting poetry as the lyrical expression of a powerful ethical and religious enlightenment. It was not Dilthey's personality as the last romantic historian which left its mark. He was more influential as an interpreter of *Geistesgeschichte,* of the universal history of mind, which embraces and governs political history, rather than parts company with it. Men like Troeltsch, Meinecke, Groethuysen, trod in his footsteps. His example was also followed in the venture of hermeneutics, the doctrine of "understanding," the attempt to define on a psychological plane the method of historical knowledge, and to extract from irrational intuition the categories of such knowledge. Spranger, Litt, Freyer, Günther, are in this respect, his cautious heirs. Finally, his theory of the types of world-views is the starting point of the *Typenlehre* which we find everywhere in German culture in the first quarter of the present century: in the psycho-typology of Spranger and Jaspers, in the "sight-forms" of Wölfflin, in Klages' theory of character, in Spengler's "morphology of cultures, in "German sociology." In fact, once history is denied real movement (*Bewegung*) and novelty, historiography must transform and fix itself into typology and sociology. For Dilthey, however, the final category of historical understanding was life itself. The types for Dilthey were only artificial structures imposed upon the history of intellectual creativeness to make it more understandable to the historian.

APPENDIX

THE DREAM[1]

I have endeavored to present methods of research to my students and have attempted to develop in them the ability to analyze reality. This power of analysis is the key to all philosophizing and historical thinking. I have no solution for the enigma of life; what I would like to transmit to my students is the temper of life which has developed in me as a result of my reflecting on the meaning of historical consciousness. This tone or temper of life I would like to express again today. But every expression is either too difficult or too cold. My friend Wildenbruch, however, has shown me a way. How deeply honored a man feels when praised by a poet! The poet Wildenbruch has called forth the poet in me and therefore he is responsible, if the ashheap begins to glow again and I attempt to express my consciousness of life which has evolved out of many years of philosophical concern. I shall not express my thoughts in verse; nevertheless, allow me some poetic license.

This happened more than a decade ago. One clear summer evening I arrived at my friend's castle, Klein-Oels. As usual our philosophical conversation lasted deep into the night, and still resounded in my mind when I undressed in the old familiar bedroom. I faced Volpato's fine etching of the School of Athens which hung over the bed. It was gratifying to visualize how the harmonious spirit of the divine Raphael blended the life and death struggle of hostile philosophical systems into a peaceful discourse. About these gentle, related figures there

[1] Wilhelm Dilthey, *"Gesammelte Schriften,"* VIII, 218-24.

hovered an atmosphere of peace which, for the first time at the dawn of ancient culture, strove to harmonize powerfully conflicting thoughts. In the noblest intellects of the Renaissance the same atmosphere was present.

Tired, I fell asleep. Instantly an alert dream life possessed me. I dreamed of Raphael's picture and of our conversation. In my dream, the figures of the philosophers came to life; in the distance, I saw on the left a long line of men, in varied garments of succeeding centuries, approach the temple of the philosophers. Whenever a philosopher passed and turned his face toward me, I tried to recognize him. There was Bruno, Descartes, Leibniz, and so many others just as I had imagined them in the light of their portraits. They ascended the steps and, as they did so, the barriers of the Temple collapsed. The newcomers mixed with the Greek philosophers. Then something happened which I did not expect even in a dream. As if driven by an inner necessity, they hastened toward each other to assemble themselves in groups. At first the movement pressed to the right where the mathematician, Archimedes, drew his circles and where the astronomer, Ptolemy, was recognizable by the globe he wore. Then there gathered all those thinkers, who based their explanation of the world upon the material solidity of the universal physical nature. Proceeding from the lower to the higher, they tried to find a single causality in the universe which could be derived from the dependent laws of nature; they subordinated the spirit to matter. They have limited our knowledge to what is known only through the methods of the natural sciences. In this group of materialists and positivists I also recognized d'Alembert with his fine features and ironic smile which seemed to mock the dreams of the metaphysicians. I also saw Comte, the systematizer of positivism, to whom a group of thinkers from all nations listened devotedly.

Another group pressed toward the center where Socrates and the noble figure of the old and god-like Plato were distinguishable. Socrates and Plato have tried to establish the knowledge of a supersensual world order based on the consciousness of the divine in the human. I also saw St. Augustine, whose heart was so passionately seeking God; around him clustered many philosophizing theologians. I listened to their conversation seeking to reconcile the idealism of personality, which is the essence of Christianity, with the teachings of the two venerable Greeks. Then Descartes separated himself from the mathematical naturalists—Descartes, whose delicate figure worn out by the power of thought was drawn as if by an inner force toward the idealists of freedom and personality. The whole circle opened as soon as the slightly stooped, slightly built Kant, his features hardened by the strain of thought, approached with his three-cornered hat and cane. This was the great Kant who elevated the idealism of freedom to the level of critical consciousness, thus reconciling it with empirical knowledge. Walking energetically toward Kant came Schiller, the poet of the idealism of freedom, whose melancholy face reflected deep thought, a poetic idealizing intuition, and the divination of his tragic fate. Fichte and Carlyle approached; Ranke, Guizot, and other great historians seemed to be listening attentively to them. A strange shudder seized me when I saw together with them a friend of my youth, Heinrich von Treitschke.

The two groups had hardly assembled when from the left converged thinkers of all nations around Pythagoras and Heracleitus, the first men to intuit the divine harmony of the universe. Giordano Bruno, Spinoza and Leibniz were also present. A wondrous spectacle, walking hand in hand as in the days of their youth, was the sight of Schelling and Hegel, our nation's greatest thinkers. All these philosophers were proclaimers of a comprehensive, spiritual divine power in the universe which lives in every object and every person, operating in them all according to the laws of nature, with the consequences that there is no transcendental order, no realm of free will. It seemed to me that all these thinkers hid poetic souls behind their furrowed faces. A commotion arose among them when, at last, with a measured step, arrived a majestic figure whose countenance was stern and composed. I was filled with reverence when I saw the large radiant eyes and the Apollonian head of Goethe. He was in the prime of life and all his creations—Faust, Wilhelm Meister, Iphigenie, and Tasso—appeared to encompass him with all his great thoughts about laws of evolution which extend from nature to the creations of man.

Amid these great men, some figures were standing, others lying down and still others restlessly moving about. These people wished to mediate: between positivism with its thorough rejection of life's enigma, and all metaphysics, but also between an all comprehensive determinism, and those who believed in the freedom of the individual. But in vain the mediators hastened to and fro among the groups. The distance between the groups increased with each moment. Now even the ground disappeared from under them and a hostile alienation enveloped them. A strange anxiety overcame me, a philosophically engendered anxiety caused by seeing philosophy divided and torn in three or even more directions. The unity of my being was torn asunder for I was deeply attracted at times to one group and at other times to the second or even to the third. I strove for the unity of thought, and in this struggle the cover of sleep became thinner and lighter, the figures of my dream faded away. And I awoke. The stars glimmered through the large windows of the room. The immeasurability and impenetrability of the universe overwhelmed me. How free I felt when I thought of the consoling ideas which I had offered to my friend in our previous evening's conversation.

This immeasurable, incomprehensible and unfathomable universe mirrors itself palpably in founders of religion, in poets and in philosophers. These all stand under the influence of time and space. Every world-view is conditioned historically and therefore limited and relative. A frightful anarchy of thought appears. The very historical consciousness that has brought forth this absolute doubt, however, is able to set limits for it. The world views are divided by an inner law. Here my thoughts returned to the three groups of philosophers of my dream. These types of world views exist along side each other through the centuries. The liberating element here is that the world views are grounded in the nature of the universe and in the relationship between the finite perceptive mind and the universe. Thus each world-view expresses within its limitations one aspect of the universe. In this respect each is true. Each, however, is one-sided. To contemplate all the aspects in their totality is denied to us. We see the pure light of truth only in various broken rays.

Philosophy has a Janus face. The unquenchable metaphysical drive aims toward the solution of the world and the enigma of life. Up to this point the philosophers are related to the men of religion and the poets. However, the philosophers are distinguished from them by desiring to solve this life enigma by a universally valid knowledge. A solution based on this presupposition is no longer possible for us.

The highest aim of philosophy is that the objective thinking of an experimental science, which derives from appearances an order determined by laws, is raised to the consciousness of itself. There is an accessible reality given in appearances, an order according to laws. This order is truth, universally valid, although expressed in the figurative speech of our senses and our faculty of perception. This basis of our knowledge is the highest object of philosophical inquiry. Toward this end, all true philosophers have worked. Another result of philosophy is the organization of empirical sciences. A philosophical spirit is present where the basis of science is simplified or sciences are related to each other, where their relation to the idea of knowledge is established, or methods are tested according to their value for the attainment of knowledge. It seems to me, however, that the time is past when there can be an independent philosophy of art, religion, law, or of the state. The powerful cohesion which is thus constituted is the highest realization of philosophy and is destined to guide the human race. The natural sciences have transformed the outer world. In the great world epoch now evolving, the social sciences are winning an ever-increasing influence.

Beyond this universally valid knowledge lie questions which are of concern for each person so alone in life and in death.

The answers to these questions are given only in the framework of the different world-views, in which our reason expresses in various forms the complexities of reality, all of which point to a single truth. This truth is hidden and each system is involved in antinomies. Historical consciousness shatters the last chains that philosophy and natural sciences could not break. Man has now achieved freedom. At the same time, however, historical consciousness saves the unity of man's soul; the glimpse into a final harmony, although otherwise incomprehensible, is revealed by the creative power of our essential being. Confidently we may recognize in each of these world views an element of truth. And if the course of our life brings us closer to a particular aspect of the incomprehensible harmony, if the truth of the world view which this particular aspect expresses fills us with creativity, then we may quietly surrender. For truth is present in them all.

These were the thoughts that arose again and again as I lay awake between dream and dream. For a long time I thought of these ideas, raising my eyes to the summer majesty of the stars. Finally a light slumber overcame me and dreams returned. The starry arches shone brighter and clearer, as the light of the morning flooded in. Light, blissful figures passed through the skies. When I awoke I strove in vain to recall the happy images of my dreams. I felt that surely these images were the expression of the bliss, of the highest freedom and of the creative activity of the soul.

This is the dream I have recorded for my friends. I hope that some of the tone and feeling of life in which my dream resounds can be transmitted to them. Stimulated more than ever, our generation seeks to read the mysterious face of life with its laughing mouth and its sad eyes. Yes, let us strive toward the light, toward freedom and beauty—but not with a new beginning, sloughing off the past. Into each new home we must take the old gods with us. In vain Nietzsche sought, in lonely self-meditation, the primordial nature and his own unhistorical existence. He peeled off one layer of skin after another, but what remained? Only an historically conditioned individual, the features of the supermen of the Renaissance. What man is, only his history tells. In vain others put the past behind them in order to begin life anew. They cannot shake off the gods of the past because they become haunting ghosts. The melody of our life is conditioned by the accompanying voices of the past. Only by surrendering to the great objective forces which history has engendered can man liberate himself from the pain of the moment and from ephemeral joy. Neither subjective caprice nor egotistic pleasure can reconcile man with life. Only surrender of his sovereign personality to the course of the world can affect this reconciliation.

SOURCES

DILTHEY'S WRITINGS

"Schleiermacher," *Westermanns Monatshefte,* V (1859), 602-14.

"Satan in der christlichen Poesie: Eine literarhistorische Studie," *Westermanns Monatshefte,* VIII (1860), 321-29, 434-39.

Aus Schleiermachers Leben in Briefen, Vols. III and IV. Edited by Dilthey. Berlin, 1860-1863.

Das Leben Schleiermachers. Berlin, 1870.

Gesammelte Schriften. 12 vols. Leipzig and Berlin, 1914-1936.

Briefwechsel zwischen Wilhelm Dilthey und dem Grafen Yorck von Wartenburg 1877-1897. Edited by Sigrid von der Schulenburg. Halle, 1923.

Das Erlebnis und die Dichtung. Leipzig and Berlin, 1929.

Von deutscher Dichtung und Musik. Leipzig and Berlin, 1933.

Der junge Dilthey: Ein Lebensbild in Briefen und Tagebüchern, 1852-1870. Edited by Clara Misch. Leipzig and Berlin, 1933.

"Briefe Wilhelm Diltheys an Bernhard und Luise Scholz, 1859-1864," in Sitzungsberichte der preussischen Akademie der Wissenschaften, Philosophisch-historische Klasse. Edited by Sigrid von der Schulenburg. Berlin, 1933.

"Briefe Wilhelm Diltheys an Rudolf Haym, 1861-1873," in Abhandlungen der preussischen Akademie der Wissenschaften, Philosophisch-historische Klasse. Edited by Erich Weniger. Berlin, 1936.

OTHER SOURCES

Antoni, Carlo. Vom Historismus zur Sociologie. Stuttgart, no date.

Aron, Raymond. Essai sur la théorie de l'histoire dans l'Allemagne Contemporaine: La Philosophie Critique de l'Histoire. Paris, 1938.

Ashton, John. Wilhelm Dilthey and his Early Critique of Historical Reason. Chicago, 1951.

Baring, Nina. Wilhelm Diltheys Philosophie der Geschichte. Freiburg, 1936.

Bischoff, Diedrich. Wilhelm Diltheys geschichtliche Lebensphilosophie. Leipzig, 1935.

Buckle, Henry Thomas. History of Civilization in England. New York, 1934.

Bullnow, O. F. Dilthey: Eine Einführung in seine Philosophie. Leipzig, 1935.

Bursian, Conrad. Geschichte der classischen Philologie in Deutschland. 2 vols. Munich and Leipzig, 1883.

Cassirer, Ernst. The Problem of Knowledge. New Haven, 1950.

Comte, Auguste. Cours de philosophie positive. 5th ed. 6 vols. Paris, 1893-1894.

Droysen, Johann Gustav. "Die Erhebung der Geschichte zum Rang einer Wissenschaft," *Historische Zeitschrift,* IX (1863), 1-22.

———— Johann Gustav Droysen: Briefwechsel. Edited by Rudolf Hübner. 2 vols. Berlin and Leipzig, 1929.

———— Johann Gustav Droysen: Historik. Edited by Rudolf Hübner. 2d ed. Munich and Berlin, 1943.

———— Politische Schriften. Edited by Felix Gilbert. Munich and Berlin, 1933.

Engel-Janosi, Friedrich. The Growth of German Historicism. Baltimore, 1944.

Groethuysen, Bernhard. "Wilhelm Dilthey," *Deutsche Rundschau,* CLIV (1913), 69-92, 249-70.

Hegel, Georg Wilhelm Friedrich. The Phenomenology of Mind. Translated and edited by J. B. Baillie. 2d ed. New York, 1931.

———— Hegel's Philosophy of Right. Translated and edited by T. M. Knox. Oxford, 1942.

———— Sämtliche Werke. Vol. VIII: Vorlesungen über die Philosophie der Weltgeschichte. Edited by Georg Lasson. Leipzig, 1920.

Heussi, Karl. Die Krisis des Historismus. Tübingen, 1932.

Hodges, H. A. Wilhelm Dilthey: An Introduction. New York, 1944.

Holborn, Hajo. "Dilthey and the Critique of Historical Reason," *Journal of the History of Ideas,* XI (1950), 93-118.

Humboldt, Wilhelm von. "Über die Aufgabe des Geschichtsschreibers," in Abhandlungen der Königlichen Akademie der Wissenschaften zu Berlin. Historische-Philologische Klasse. 1820-21. Berlin, 1822.

Kant, Immanuel. Immanuel Kants Werke. Edited by Ernst Cassirer. Vols. III and V. Berlin, 1914-1922.

Lazarus, Moritz. "Über den Ursprung der Sitten," *Zeitschrift für Völkerpsychologie und Sprachwissenschaft,* I (1860), 437-77.

———— "Über die Ideen in der Geschichte," *Zeitschrift für Völkerpsychologie und Sprachwissenschaft,* III (1865), 385-486.

Lessing, Gotthold Ephraim. Gotthold Ephraim Lessings sämtliche Schriften. 12 vols. Berlin, 1839.

Masur, Gerhard. "Wilhelm Dilthey und die europäische Geistesgeschichte," *Deutsche Vierteljahresschrift für Literatur und Geistesgeschichte,* XII (1934), 479-503.

Meinecke, Friedrich. Die Entstehung des Historismus, 2 vols. Munich, 1936.

Merz, John Theodore. A History of European Thought in the Nineteenth Century. 4 vols. Edinburgh and London, 1896-1914.

Mill, John Stuart. A System of Logic, Ratiocinative and Inductive. New York. 1873.

Misch, Georg. "Einleitung," in Wilhelm Dilthey, Gesammelte Schriften, Vol. V. Leipzig and Berlin, 1925.

——— Vom Lebens- und Gedankenreis Wilhelm Diltheys. Frankfort, 1947.

Nohl, Herman. "Der junge Dilthey," *Germanisch-romanische Monatsschrift,* XXII (1934), 139-44.

Ranke, Leopold von. Sämtliche Werke. Edited by Albert Dove. 54 vols. 3d ed. Leipzig, 1881-1890.

Rothacker, Erich. Einleitung in die Geisteswissenschaften. Tübingen, 1920.

Schmidt, Heinrich. Philosophisches Wörterbuch. Leipzig. 1931.

Schnabel, Franz. Deutsche Geschichte im neunzehnten Jahrhundert. Vol. I. Freiburg, 1947.

Spranger, Eduard. "Einleitung" to Sigrid von der Schulenburg, ed., "Briefe Wilhelm Diltheys an Bernhard und Luise Scholz, 1859-1864," in Sitzungberichte der preussischen Akademie der Wissenschaften. Philosophisch-Historische Klasse. Berlin, 1933.

Treitschke, Heinrich von. Heinrich von Treitschkes Briefe. Edited by Max Cornicelius, 3 vols. Leipzig, 1912-1920.

——— Historische und politische Aufsätze. 4 vols. Leipzig, 1886-1897.

——— Naturrecht auf dem Grunde der Ethik. 2d ed. Leipzig, 1868.

Trendelenburg, Adolf. Logische Untersuchungen. 2 vols. 3rd ed. Leipzig, 1870.

Troeltsch, Ernst. Gesammelte Schriften. Vol. III: Der Historismus und seine Probleme. Tübingen, 1922.

——— "Die Krisis des Historismus," *Die Neue Rundschau,* XXXIII (1922), 572-90.

Wach, Joachim. Die Typenlehre Trendelenburgs und ihr Einfluss auf Dilthey. Tübingen, 1926.

——— Das Verstehen: Grundzüge einer Geschichte der hermeneutischen Theorie im 19 Jahrhundert. 3 vols. Tübingen, 1926-1933.

INDEX